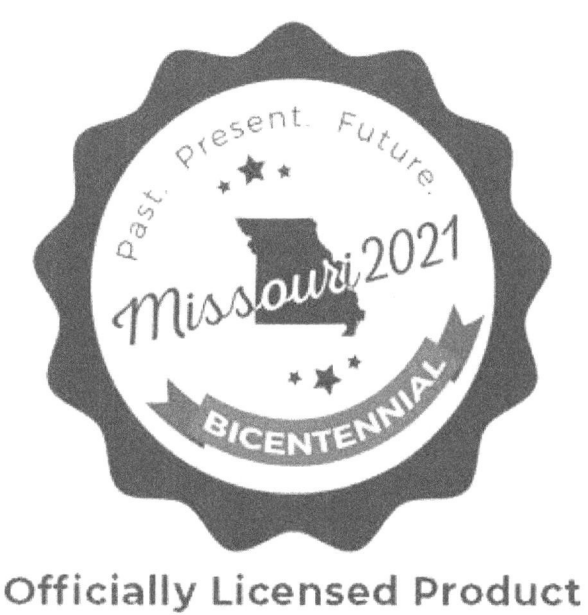

Officially Licensed Product

All proceeds from the sale of this book will go to the
MAEA High School Senior Art Teacher Scholarship Fund.

"We don't make mistakes, just happy little accidents"~ **Bob Ross**.

"Show Me Art Coloring Book" Edition 1

Copyright ©2021 Missouri Art Education Association

Art Credits: Missouri Schools Art Students

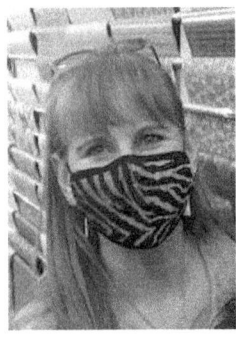

Editor Cheryl Church

Carthage R9 High School Art Teacher
Former Missouri District 9 Representative, Former Missouri Secondary Representative
Conference Co-Chair 2021, 2023
Arthur / Illustrator of "The Perfect Escape" A Whimsical Odd World of Cheryl Church,
        "The Perfect Escape, Visionary & Fantasy", **coloring book.**
        "The Perfect Escape" Route 66, **coloring book and stories series.**
        "The Perfect Escape Arizona Route 66", **coloring book and stories series.**
        "The Perfect Escape Kansas Route 66" coloring book and stories series.

ISBN- 9798713085100

"Show Me Art Coloring Book"
by Missouri Art Students
1st Edition

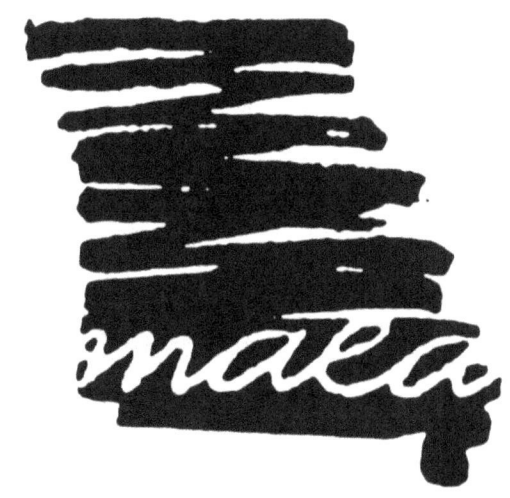

Assembled and Edited by Cheryl Church

MAEA

Missouri Art Education Association

Meaningful Art Experiences for All

It is the mission of the Missouri Art Education Association to locally, regionally, and nationally promote, preserve, and perpetuate visual art education.

- Promoting lifelong visual arts education at all levels: early childhood, K-12, higher education, museum education, and adult/community programs

- Providing art teachers opportunities for receiving collegial support and networking

- Providing our members with knowledge of and access to resources which support art education

- Working toward alignment of community, state, and national art education initiatives

- Encouraging the aesthetics inherent in the making of art

- Collaborating with all members of the learning organization

- Promoting public awareness of the knowledge, skills, and emotive aspects that are components of quality visual arts education

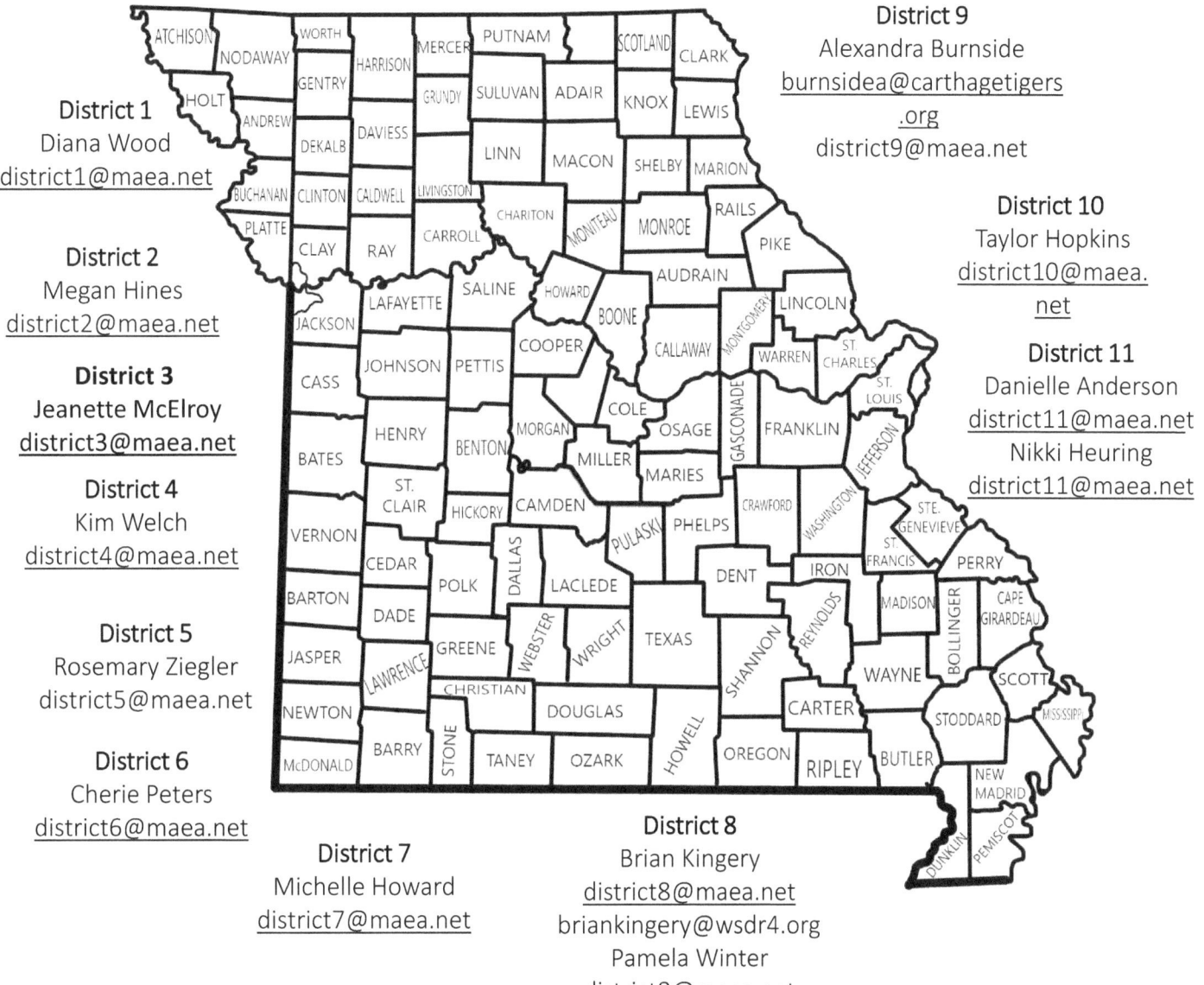

District 1
Diana Wood
district1@maea.net

District 2
Megan Hines
district2@maea.net

District 3
Jeanette McElroy
district3@maea.net

District 4
Kim Welch
district4@maea.net

District 5
Rosemary Ziegler
district5@maea.net

District 6
Cherie Peters
district6@maea.net

District 7
Michelle Howard
district7@maea.net

District 8
Brian Kingery
district8@maea.net
briankingery@wsdr4.org
Pamela Winter
district8@maea.net

District 9
Alexandra Burnside
burnsidea@carthagetigers.org
district9@maea.net

District 10
Taylor Hopkins
district10@maea.net

District 11
Danielle Anderson
district11@maea.net
Nikki Heuring
district11@maea.net

District # 1   Counties include: Andrew, Atchison, Buchanan, Caldwell, Carroll, Clay, Clinton, Davies, DeKalb, Gentry, Grundy, Harrison, Holt, Livingston, Mercer, Nodaway, Platte, Ray and Worth.

District #2   Counties include: Adair, Chariton, Clark, Knox, Lewis, Linn, Macon, Putnam, Randolph, Schuyler, Scotland, Shelby, and Sullivan.

District #3   Counties include: Kansas City Metropolitan Area

District #4   Counties include: Bates, Benton, Cass, Cooper, Henry, Hickory, Jackson, Johnson, Lafayette, Moniteau, Morgan, Pettis, Saline, and St. Clair

District #5   Counties include: Audrain, Boone, Callaway, Howard, Lincoln, Marion, Monroe, Montgomery, Pike, Ralls, and Warren

District #6   Counties include: Camden, Cole, Crawford, Dent, Gasconade, Maries, Miller, Osage, Phelps, and Pulaski.

District #7   Counties include: Franklin, Jefferson, St. Francios, St. Genevieve, and Washington.

District #8   Counties include: St. Louis City, St. Louis, and St. Charles

District #9   Counties include: Barry, Barton, Cedar, Dade, Jasper, Lawrence, McDonald, Newton, and Vernon.

District #10   Counties include: Christian, Dallas, Douglas, Greene, Howell, Laclede, Oregon, Ozark, Polk, Stone, Taney, Texas, Webster and Wright

District #11   Counties include: Bollinger, Butler, Carter, Cape Girardeau, Dunklin, Iron, Madison, Mississippi, Pemiscot, Perry, Reynolds, Ripley, Scott, Shannon, Stoddard, and Wayne.

Officers

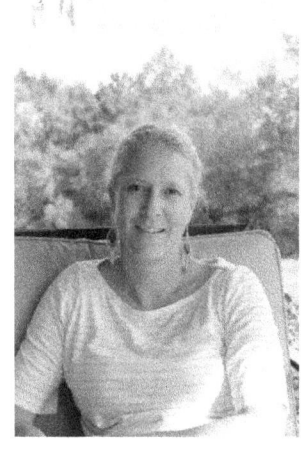

Hester Menier
President@maea.net

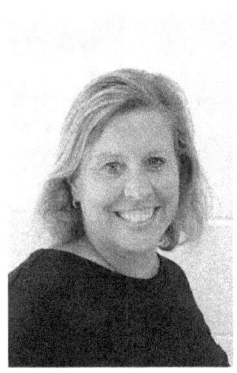

Tina Hyde
Past-President

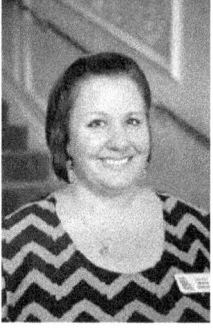

Melanie Robinson
Secretary

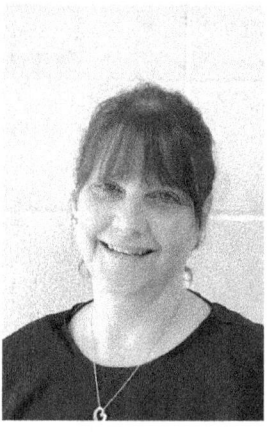

Kim Powell
President Elect
Workshop Coordinator
Executive Council

Diana Mahoney
Registration Chair
Treasurer

The Missouri Art Education Association is governed by a set of elected officers, 11 District Representatives, and 9 Division Representatives. The council is also served by several nonvoting members who are a part of standing committees and task forces. Elections are held for Council positions every two years. Contact Shannon Engelbrecht if you are would like to run for office.

MAEA Division Representatives

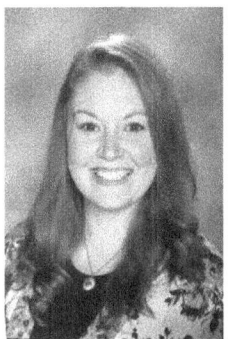

Jessie Bayless
Elementary

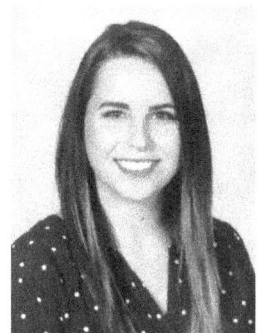

Lauren Schlesselmann
Middle

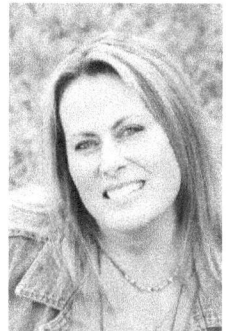

Jennifer Leeper
Secondary

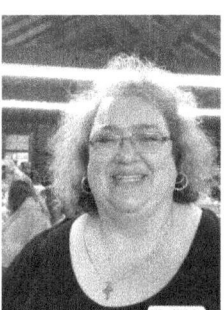

Kathy Grajek
K-12
Silent Auction

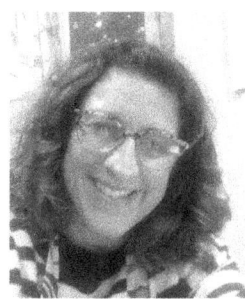

Amber Mintert
Higher Education

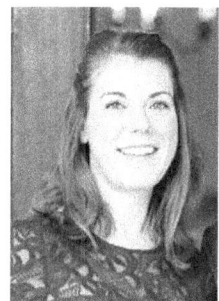

Bonnie Thomas
Museum

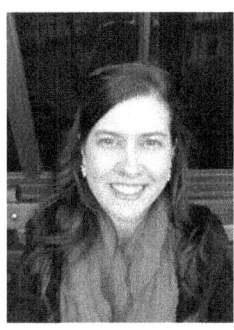

Michelle Ridlen
Supervision/Administration

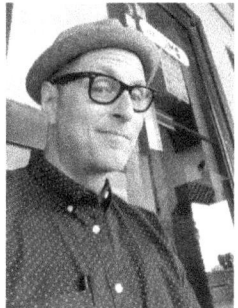

Chris Mostyn
Student/First 5

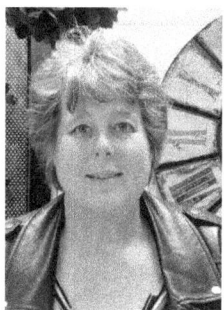

Debra Straatmann
Retired Representative

(not pictured) Erin Price - YAM Flag Competition

The Missouri Art Education Association is governed by a set of elected officers, including the Executive Committee, 11 District Representatives, and 9 Division Representatives. The council is also served by several nonvoting members who are a part of standing committees and task forces. Elections are held for Council positions every two years.

Membership

The Missouri Art Education Association is Affiliated with the **National Art Education Association.** Therefore, membership in MAEA includes membership to the national organization. Visit their website for links to art education resources and advocacy, as well as national conference information.
contact Sarah Luttrell, Membership Chair. – membership@maea.net

Benefits of MAEA Membership

As a member of the largest Professional Learning Community for Visual Art Educators in Missouri, you will gain access to a wealth of art education and advocacy resources via a network of visual arts professionals. MAEA provides an opportunity to attend two state conferences each year, one in the fall and one in the spring. These are a great way to earn your content area PD hours! Members also receive our bi-annual state publication, *Show Me ART.*

Benefits of NAEA Membership

- Art Education Journals and Publications
- Free Online Professional Learning Opportunities
- My NAEA, an online resource
- National Convention
- Member Directory
- Member Discounts
- Grants, Awards, and Institutes
- Eligibility to establish a National Art Honor Society chapter in your MS/HS

Representing Missouri Schools

Salem High School, Salem, Missouri
Monett High School, Monett, Missouri
Carthage Senior High School, Carthage, Missouri
Sparta High School, Sparta Missouri
New Madrid County Central, New Madrid, Missouri
Carl Junction High School, Carl Junction, Missouri
S.C.O.R.E. of Nixa Public Schools, Nixa, Missouri
Waynesville High School, Waynesville, Missouri
Disney Elementary, Springfield, Missouri
Richland R-IV Elementary, Richland, Missouri
Truman High School, Independence, Missouri
Neosho High School, Neosho, Missouri
Troy Buchanan High School, Troy, Missouri
Marshfield High School, Marshfield, Missouri
Cole Camp High School, Cole Camp, Missouri

Missouri

The Show Me State
Salus populi suprema Lex Esto
"Let the welfare of the people be the supreme law"

Missouri obtained its name from the Missouri Indians that lived along the what is now called the Missouri river.

It was established as the 24th state of the Union in 1821.

The captivating Blue bird became Missouri's state bird in 1927 just a year after Route 66 became a road.

The state flower, Hawthorn, surrounds the grounds of the capital of Missouri, Jefferson City.

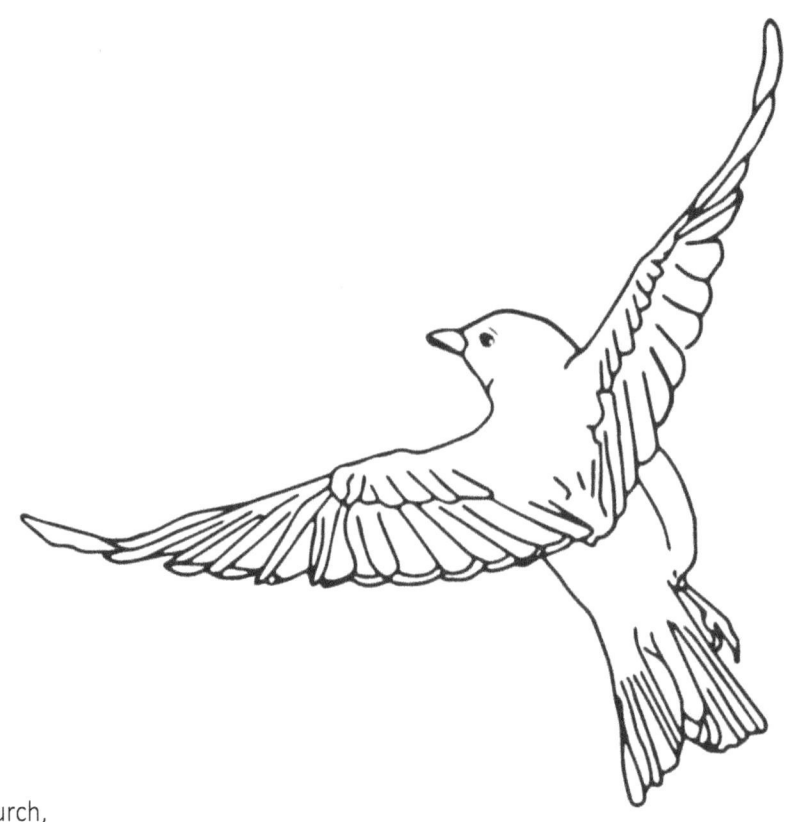

Following Illustration by Cheryl Church,
Coordinator of Show Me Art Coloring Book
Carthage R9 District High School

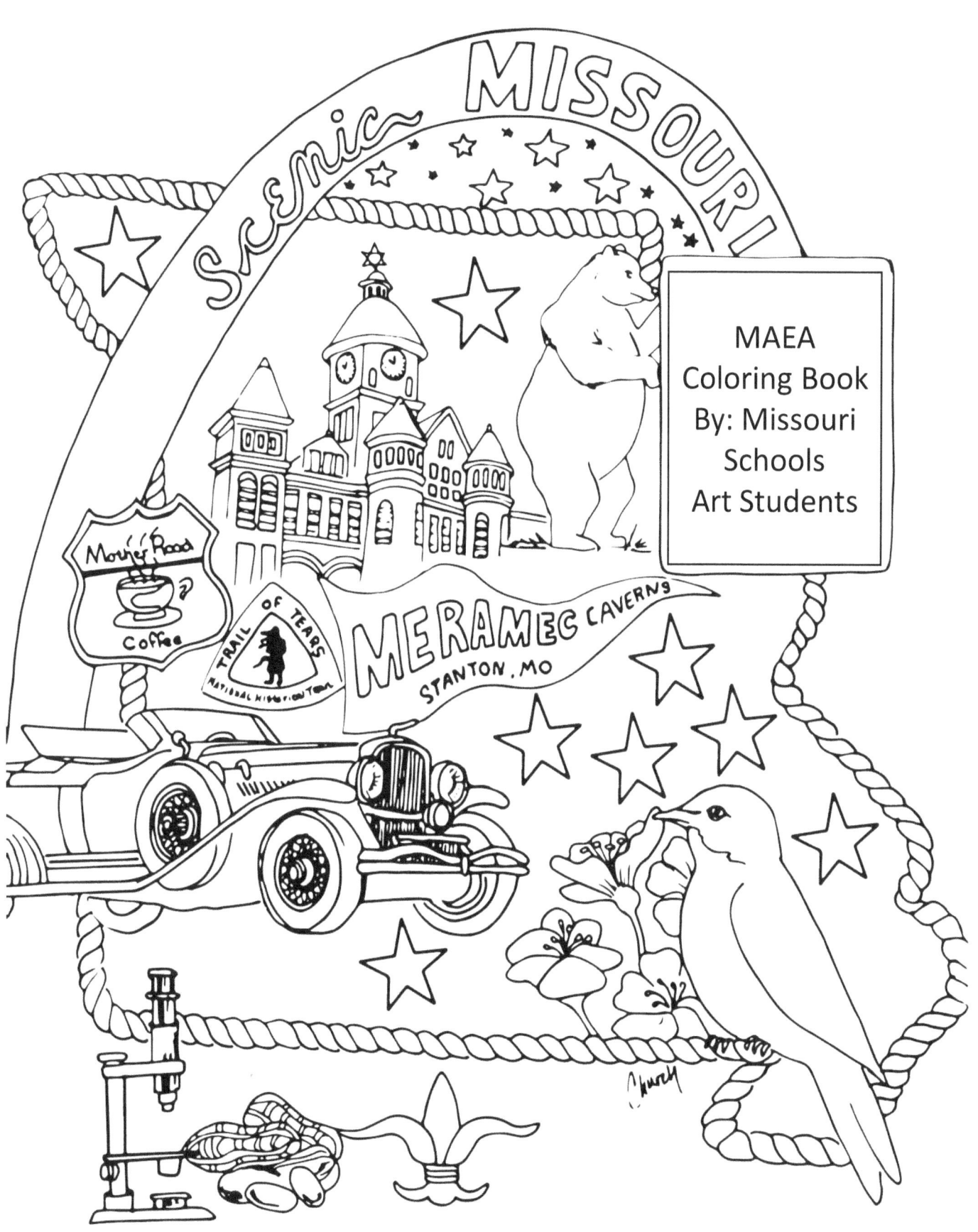

SCENIC MISSOURI

MAEA
Coloring Book
By: Missouri
Schools
Art Students

Mother Road Coffee

TRAIL OF TEARS
NATIONAL HISTORIC TRAIL

MERAMEC CAVERNS
STANTON, MO

Front cover

MAEA would like to thank Adrian Bittner for the use of their artwork for the 2021 Edition of "Show Me Art Coloring Book" Edition 1

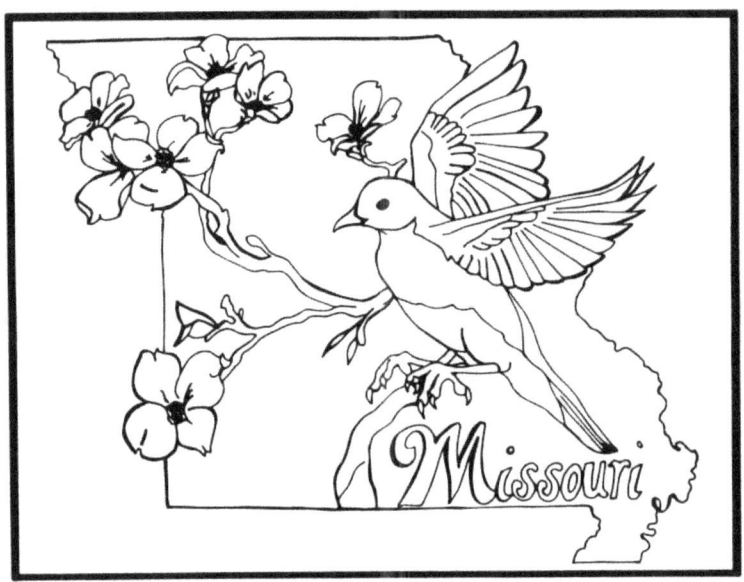

Adrian Bittner

"State Bird"
12th grade
Carl Junction
Nellie Mitchell

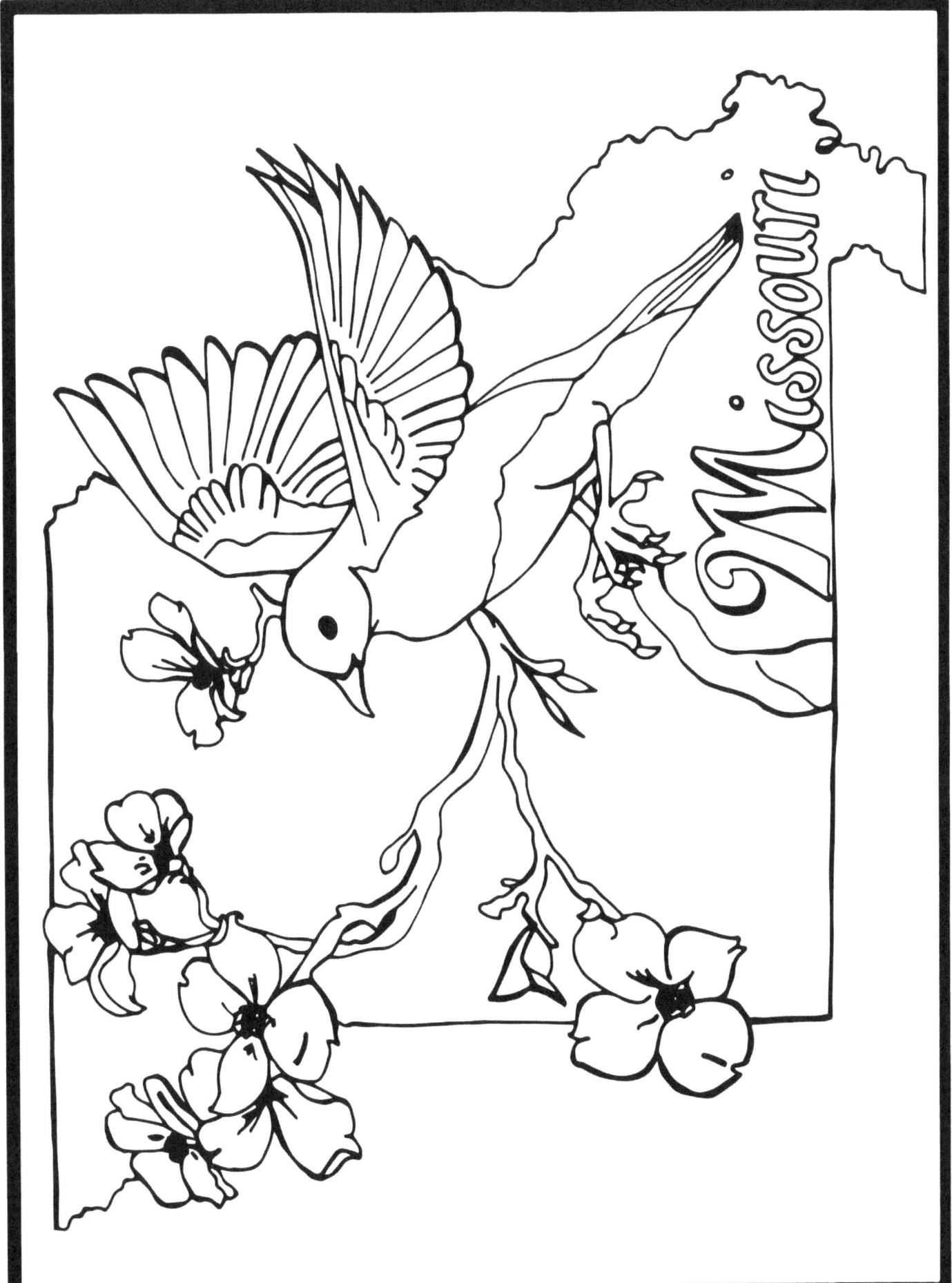

"Gateway to the West"

Kullen Myers
Senior
Teacher: Tana Kettner
Salem High School, Salem, Missouri

Artist statement:

    We visited the St. Louis Arch with our art club last year and I was so impressed with the reflective surfaces and angles. This drawing is inspired by my feelings when standing beneath the massive metal structure. I am proud of this symbol of the "gateway into the west", and the country it represents!

"Art is not what you see, but what you make others see." **Edgar Degas**

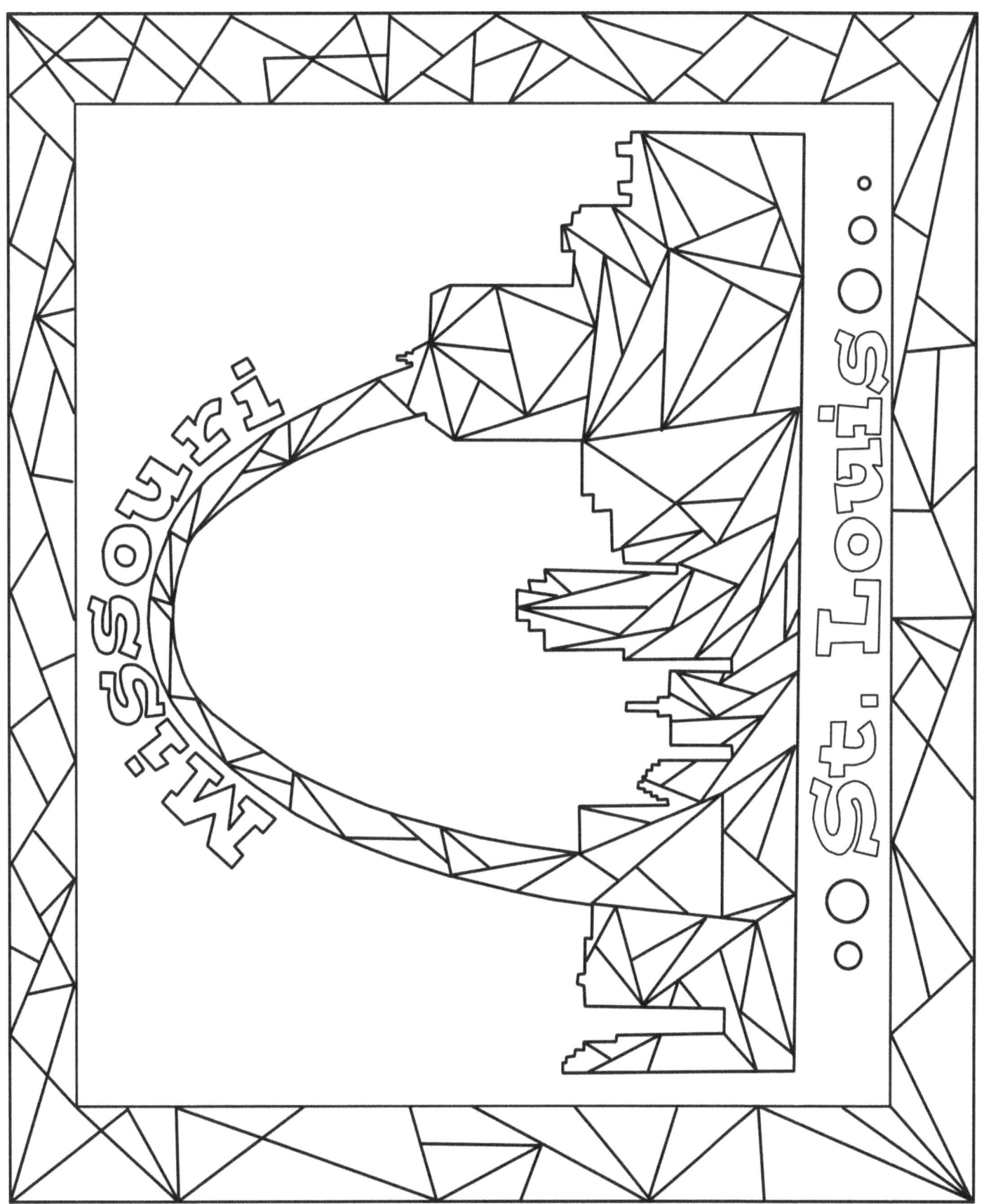

"Missouri Wildflowers"

Kullen Myers
Senior
Teacher: Tana Kettner
Salem, Missouri

Artist statement:

Although the Dogwood is Missouri's state flower, there are many other beautiful wildflowers that adorn our great state! This flower design was inspired by my grandmother's flower garden and represents the beauty of many areas in our state. I can imagine it colored with various hues of light and dark greens, yellows, blues, pinks, etc.

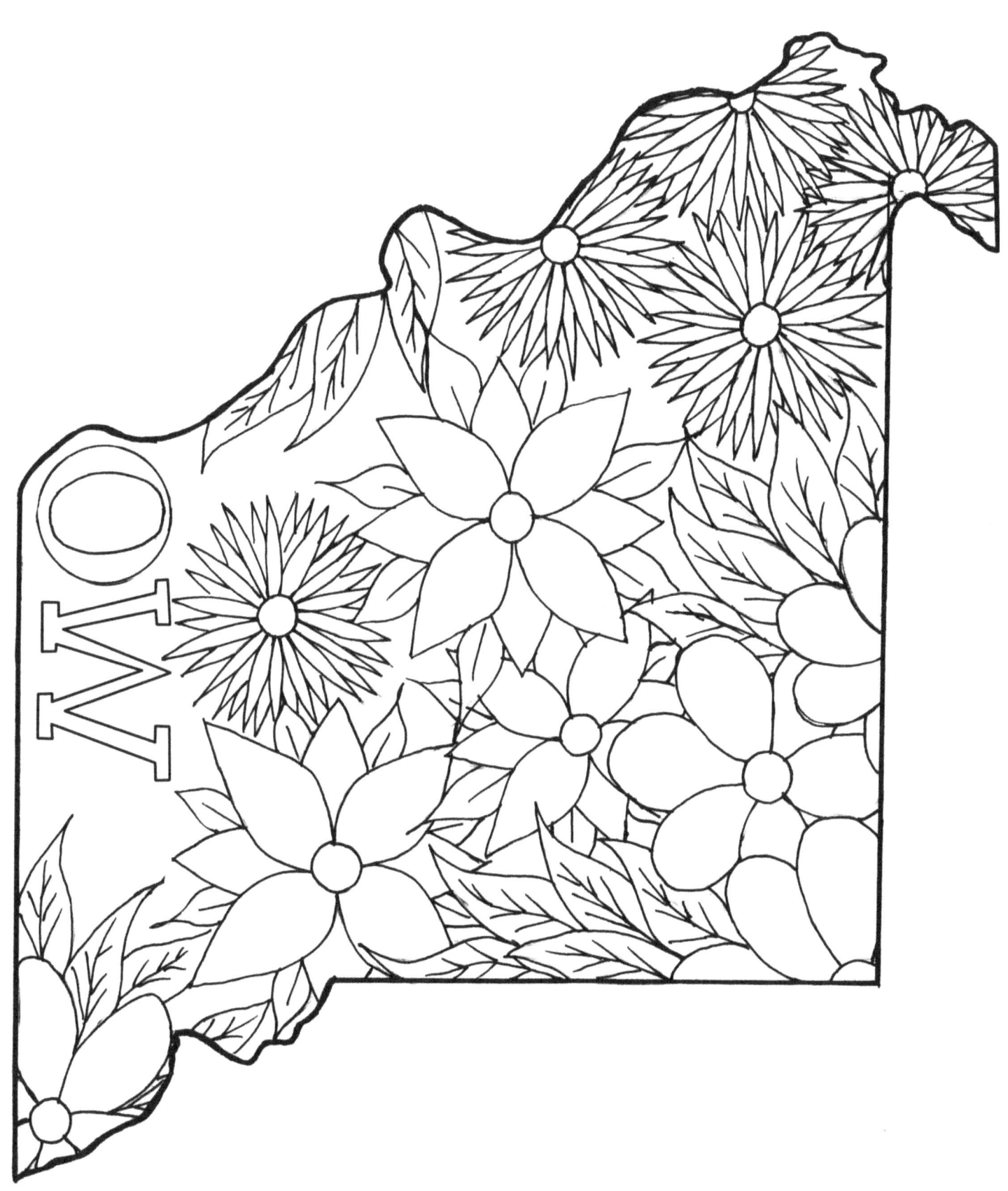

"Silver Dollar Polaroid"

Lorna Conaway
Sophomore
Monett R1
Monett, Missouri
Teacher: Mrs. Lynn Morin

Artist statement:

This piece was inspired by the experiences of some of my friends that have been to Silver Dollar City. Polaroids are a fun and popular way of capturing experiences in a way that can fit perfectly in a travel log or scrapbook, so I decided to draw an image of someone just as they enter the iconic place.

"I am seeking. I am striving. I am in it with all my heart." **Vincent van Gogh**

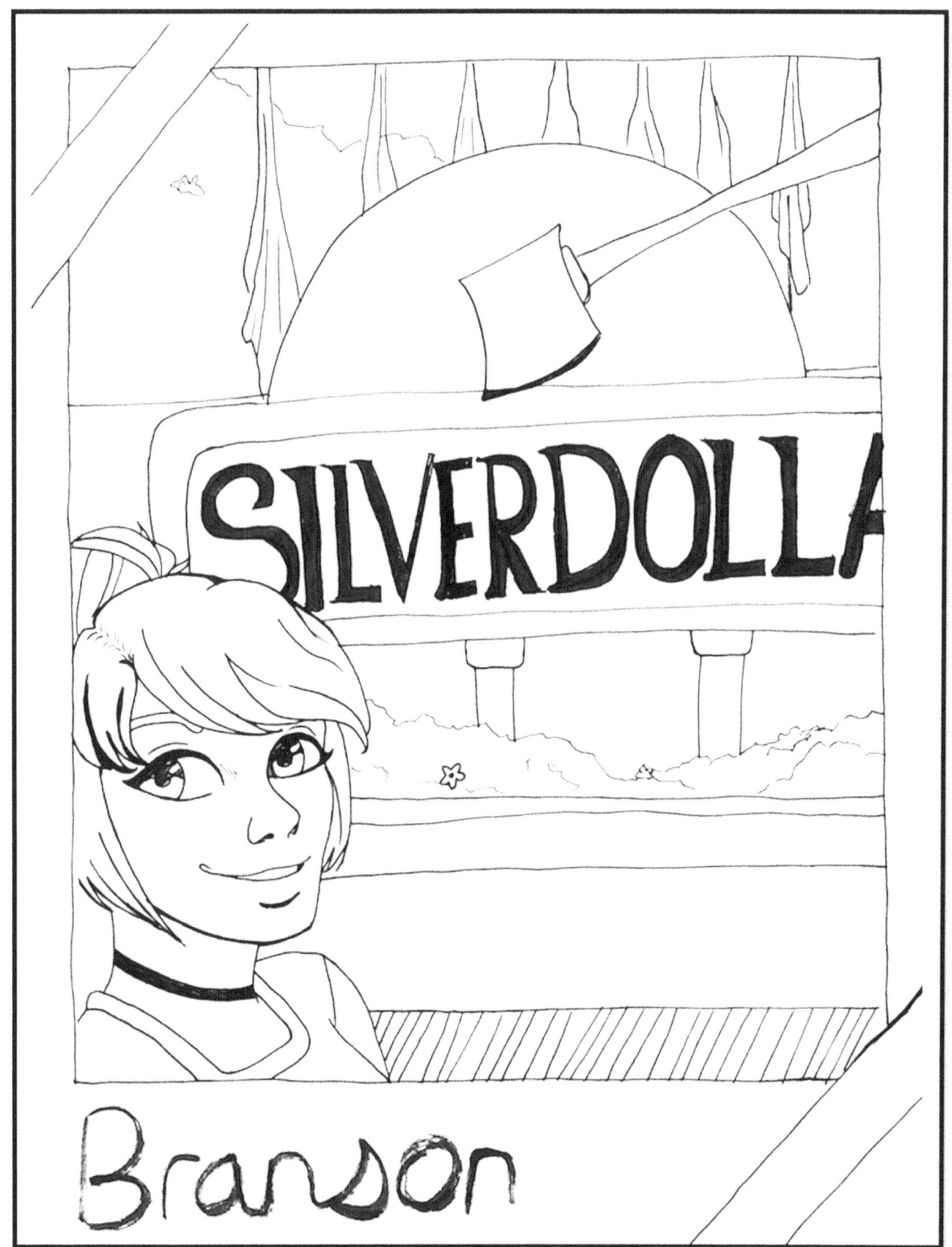

Branson

"Be Who You Are Inside and Out."

Cameron Williamson
6th Grade

Teacher Mrs. Cherie Peters
Richland R-IV Elementary
Richland, Missouri

Be Who YOU are inside and Out!

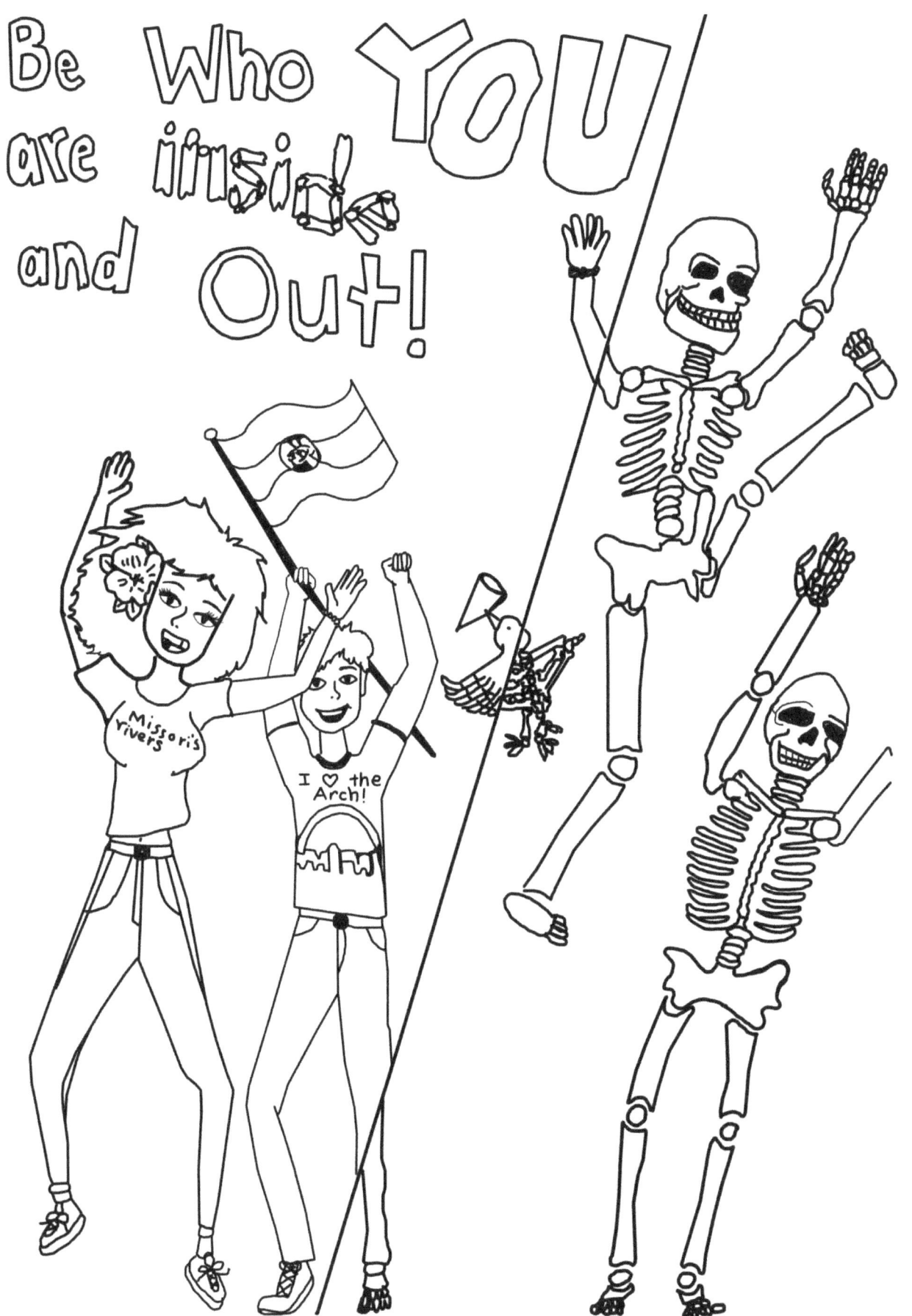

"Jesse James Wanted Poster"

Dalton Russell

Artist statement:
I chose to do Jessie James because I really like to do art of characters over things like landscapes and still life, so I picked a historical figure to draw.

Teacher: Mrs. Morin
Monett High School
Monett, Missouri

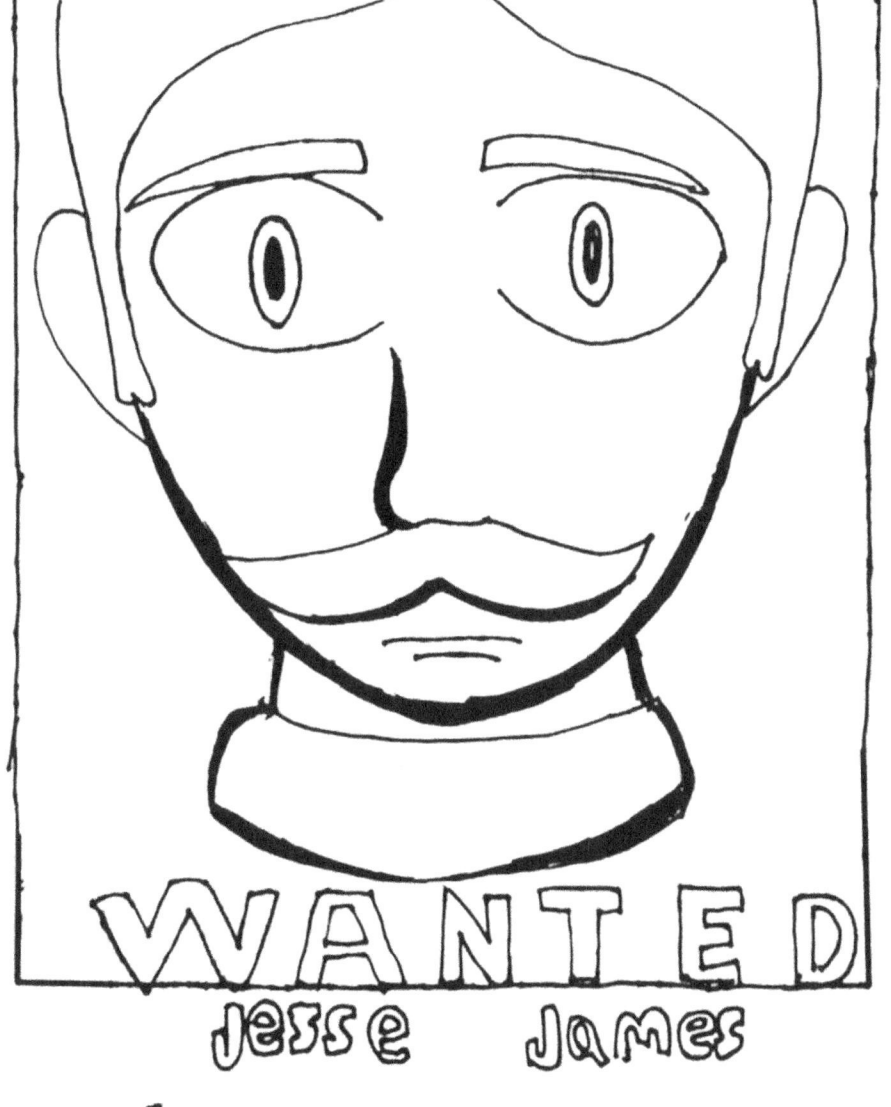

Mo° Nature

Shellsy Legorreta
Senior 2020

Artist statement:

To be completely honest I didn't know what to do when my class was presented with the assignment but I was excited for the challenge. My first thought was to draw Bonnie and Clyde, but everyone was doing that. I started off drawing our state bird the Eastern Bluebird, resting on a branch. And I got stuck their with a bird on y page and thought it would be a good transition if I did more branches and had white Hawthorns, our state flower, coming from them in every which direction.

Teacher: Cheryl Church
Carthage Senior High School
Carthage, Missouri

"Creativity takes courage" ~ *Henri Matisse.*

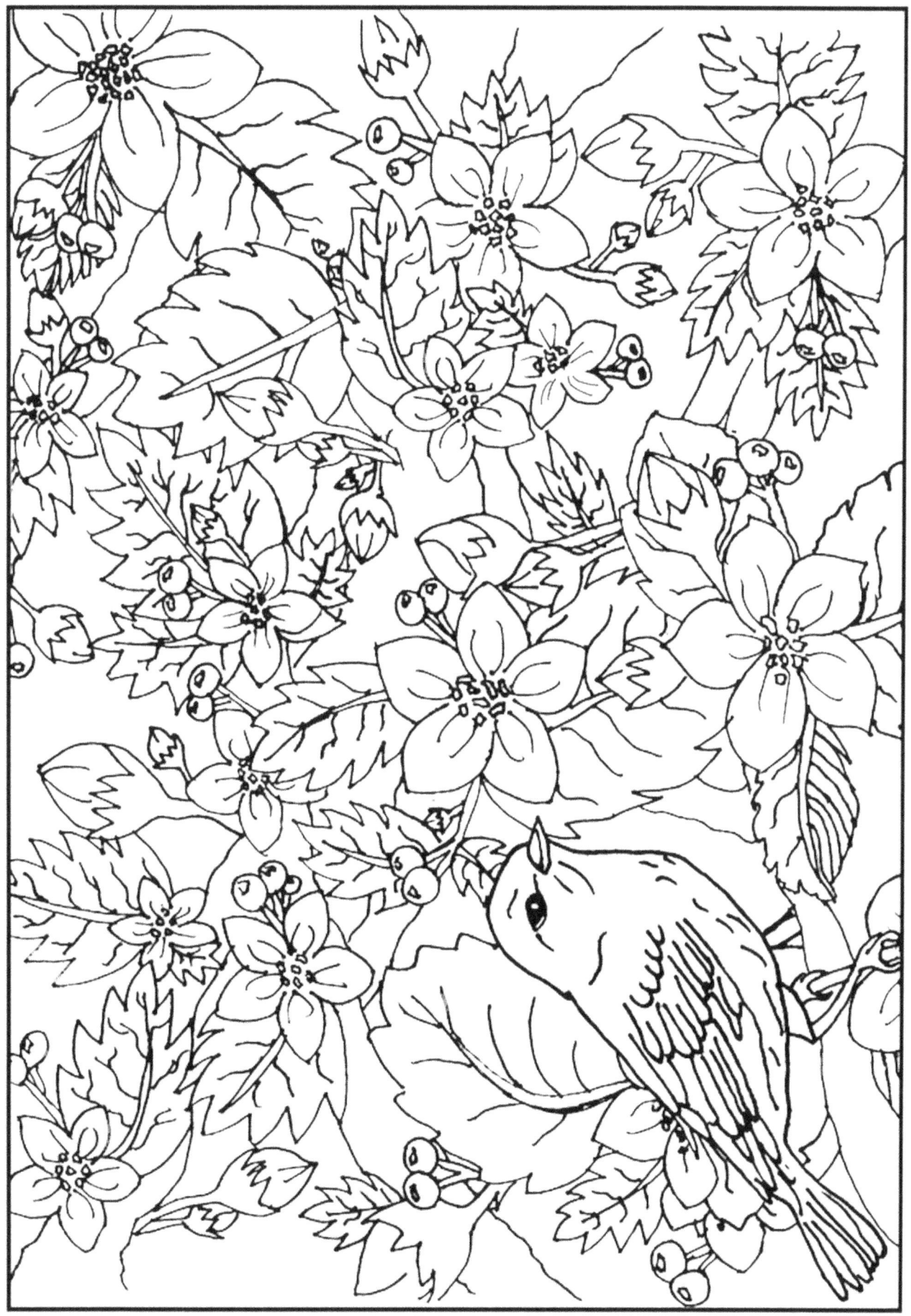

"The Bees Knees"

Zoe Gilbert

Junior

Artist statement:
The Missouri insect is a honeybee, an insect that as of 2019, is still on the endangered species list. I made this somewhat abstract coloring page as a tribute to the honeybee, one of the most important insects in our environment.

Teacher: Lynn Morin
Monett High School
Monett, Missouri

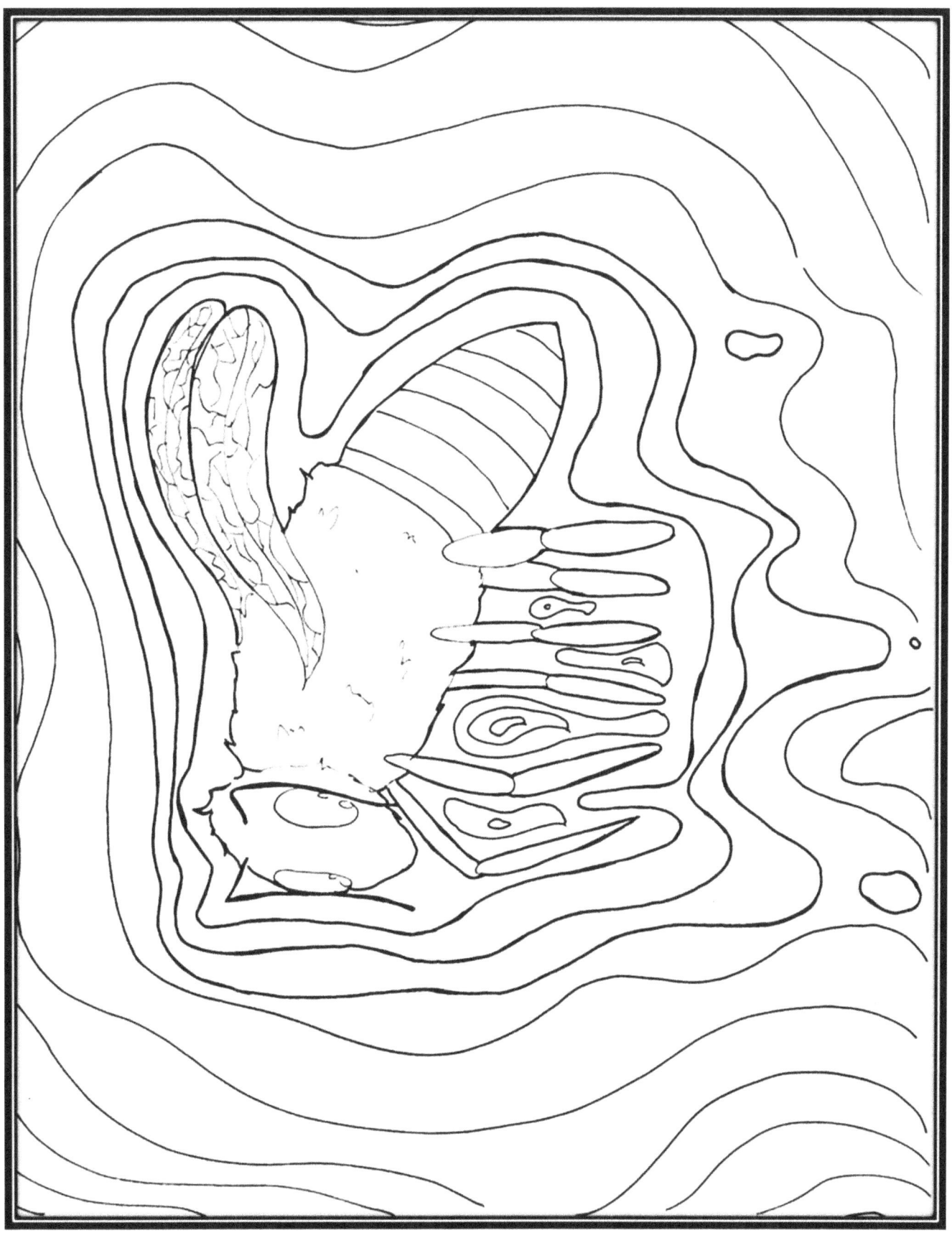

"Nature's Beauty"

Amy Tsai
Junior

Artist statement:

    This piece is a cross section of Missouri's ecosystem. I made this piece by gathering ideas that represented Missouri, and then I made a couple of sketches. I chose the best one shat suited Missouri to outline with a black marker. The idea that I wanted to portray in my art was Missouri's nature and wildlife like the channel catfish, deer, rocky soil, hills, and the abundant trees. Missouri is filled with beautiful organisms, plants, and animals, so many Missourians spend their time outside fishing, camping, and hunting. My goal for this piece was to create something that would catch the attention of tourist to take the time to no only enjoy the popular landmarks of Missouri but also the natural wildlife that we have to offer. Overall, this piece was very well portrayed, and it provides a simple outline for one to add the natural colors of Missouri.

Teacher: Mrs. Morin
Monett R1 High School
Monett, Missouri

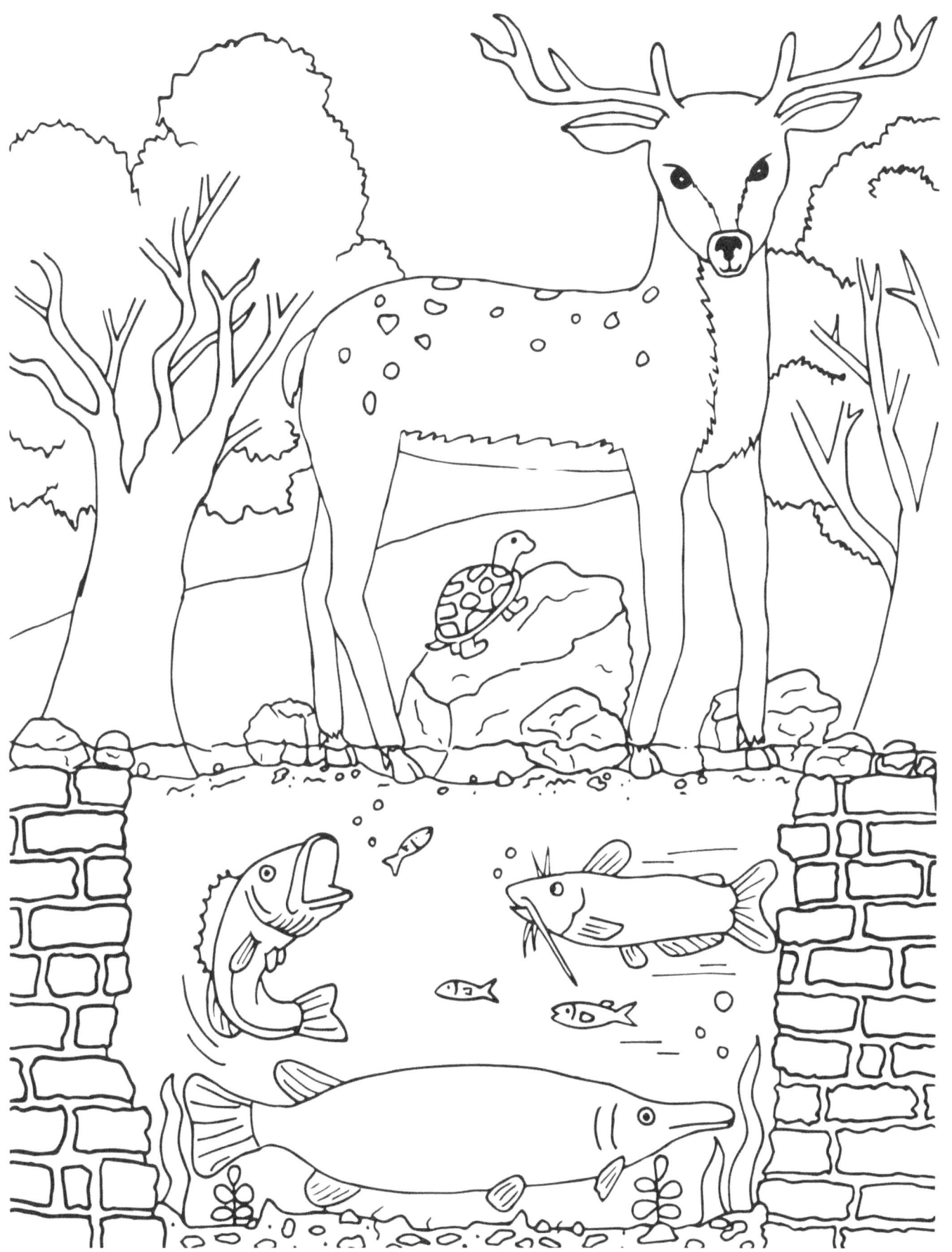

"Sialia Sialis"

Aveline McEntire
Junior

Artist statement:
The Eastern Bluebird is Missouri's state bird. It is beautiful in a simplistic way, and represents the spirit of the lifestyle of this state. I wanted to show that by keeping the design mostly simple, yet beautiful. I also left the background blank to give the freedom of creating your own background, symbolizing how you can **color your life whatever way you want, no matter the template in front of you.**

Teacher : Lynn Morin
Monett High School
Monett, Missouri

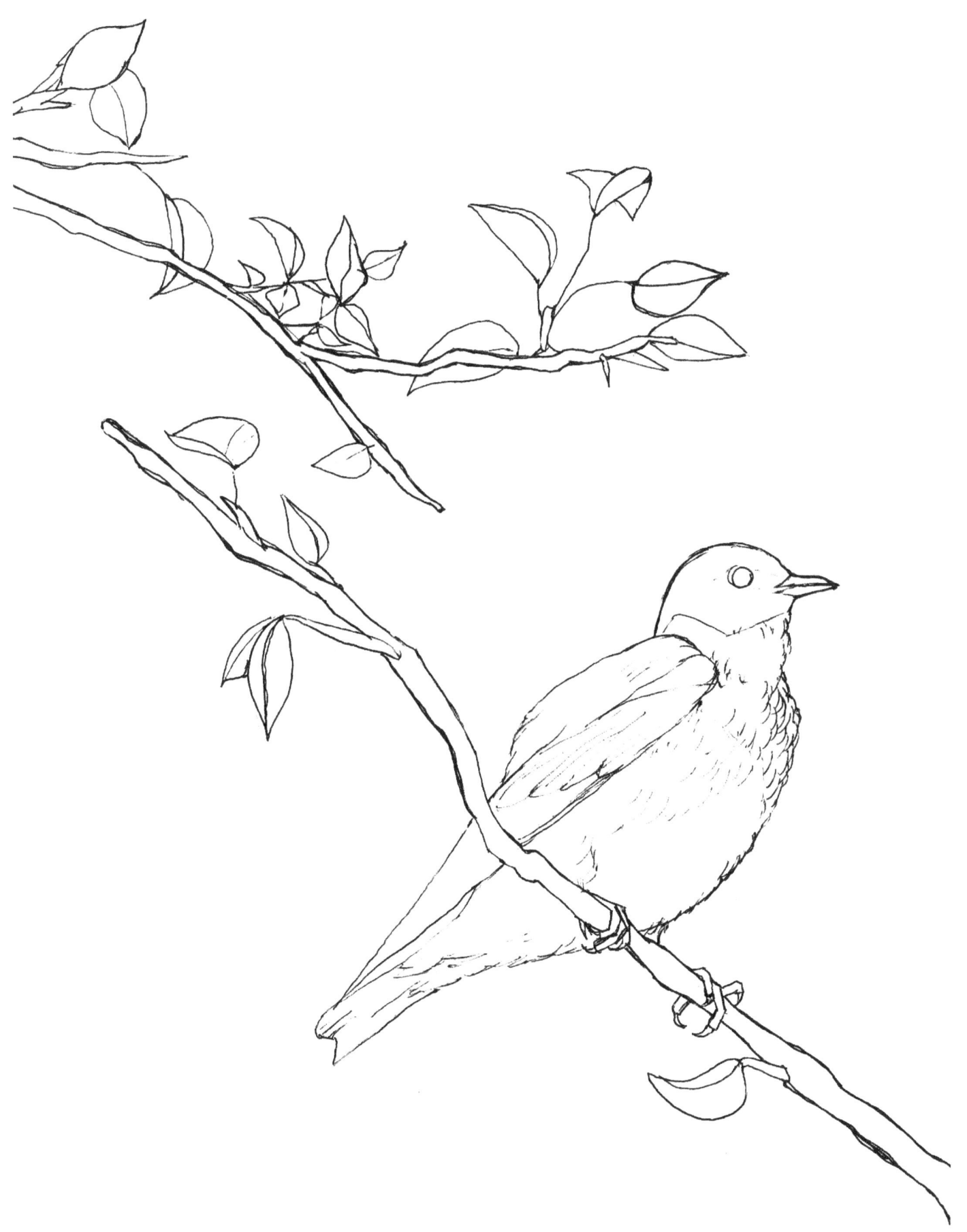

Missouri Wildlife

Cecilia Thomas
Age 16

For my artwork I wanted to highlight Missouri's diverse and beautiful wildlife. I drew some of the Missouri's mammals and also included the state bird, a bluebird, and Missouri's state tree, the flowering Dogwood.

Teacher: Stephanie Pate
Cole Camp High School
Cole Camp, Missouri

MISSOURI

wildlife

Eastern
Bluebird

Eastern
Grey Squirrel

white-tailed
deer

Coyote

Northern
Raccoon

"The Crataegus Blue Bird"

Euler Oxlaj
Senior 2021

Artist statement:
I thought that the Eastern Bluebird would be a nice because it represents Missouri how it's soaring through the skies. I seen many pictures of it next to trees and I thought the flowers would be nice seeing that the flowers would show that it look like one with the bird. I thought it was a nice way saying welcome to Missouri.

Cheryl Church
Carthage R9. Carthage

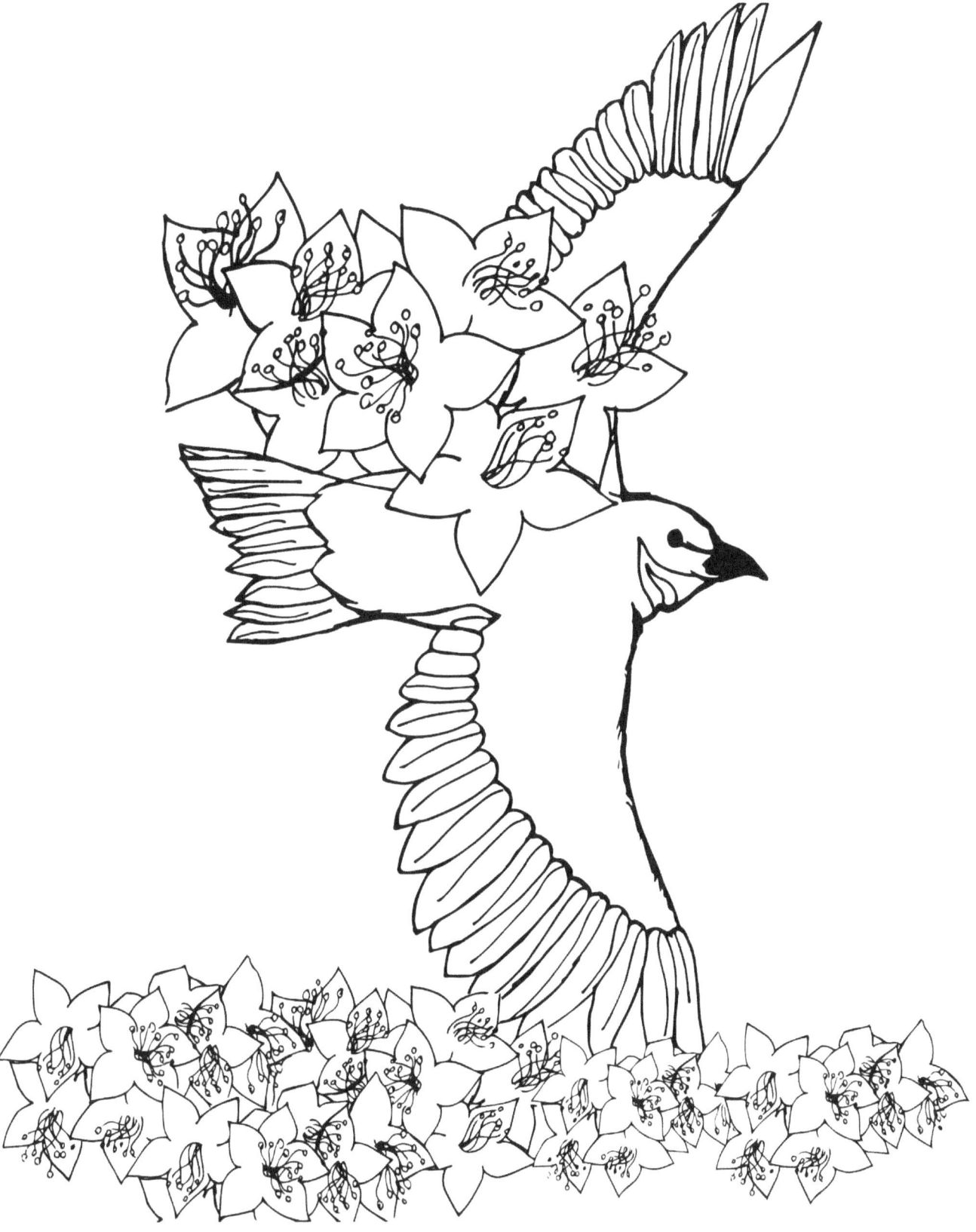

"Ted Drews"

Nancy Campa
Junior

Artist Statement:

Teacher: Cheryl Church
Carthage R-9, Carthage

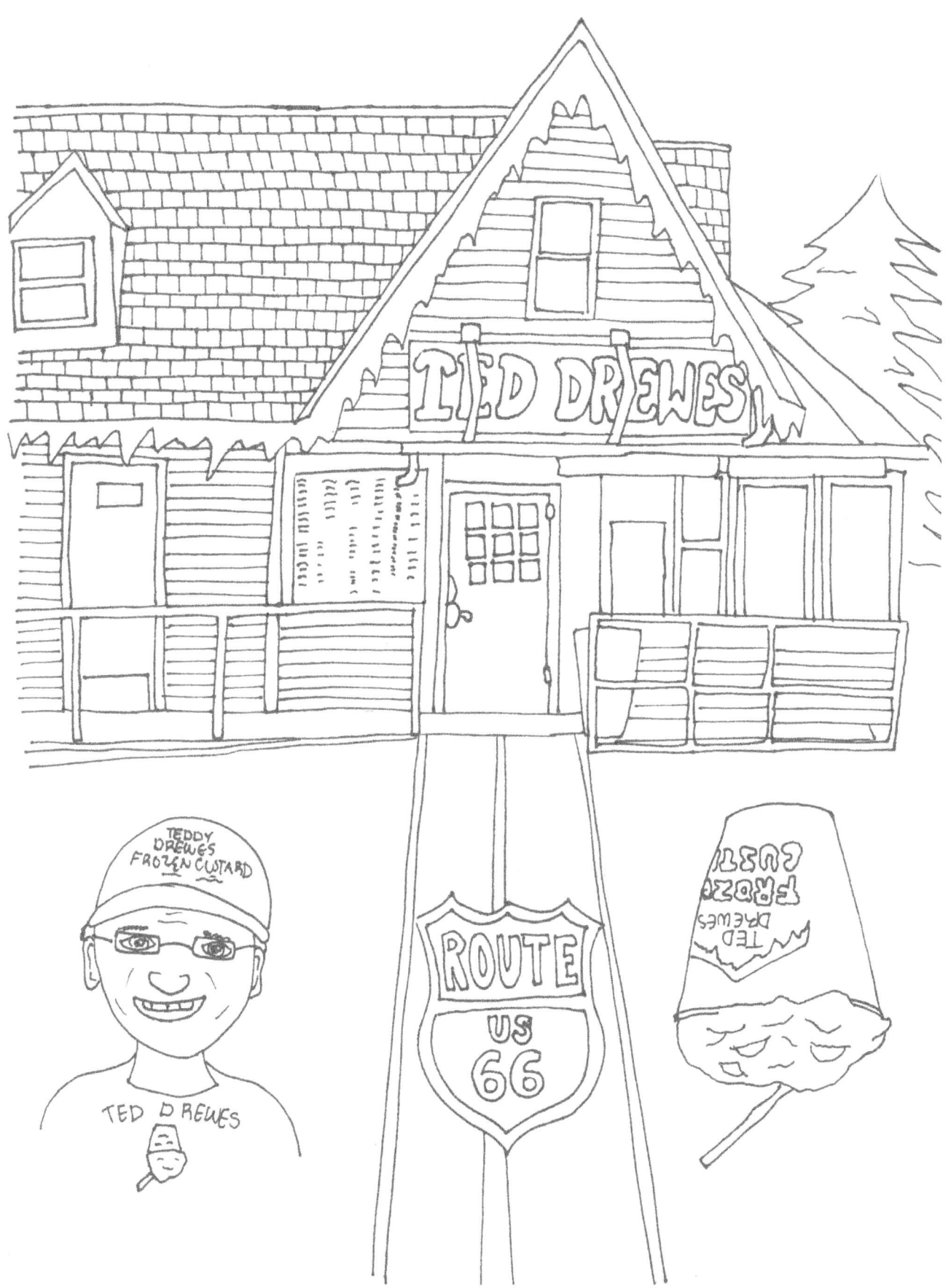

"Mark My Words"

Justin Sneed
Senior 2021

Description: I thought of a famous Missourian, Mark Twain, then I thought of a popular city in Missouri which led to the creation of my artwork.

Teacher: Cheryl Church
Carthage R-9
Carthage, Missouri

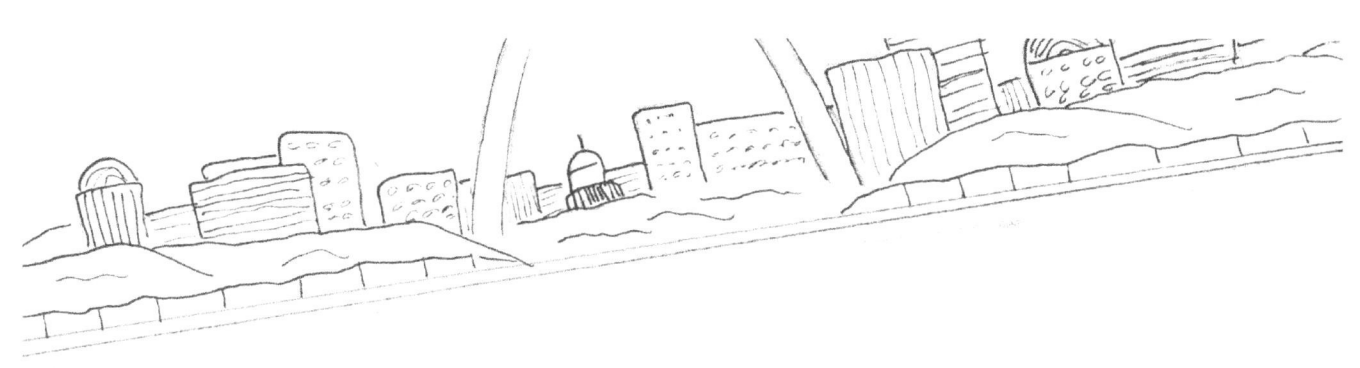

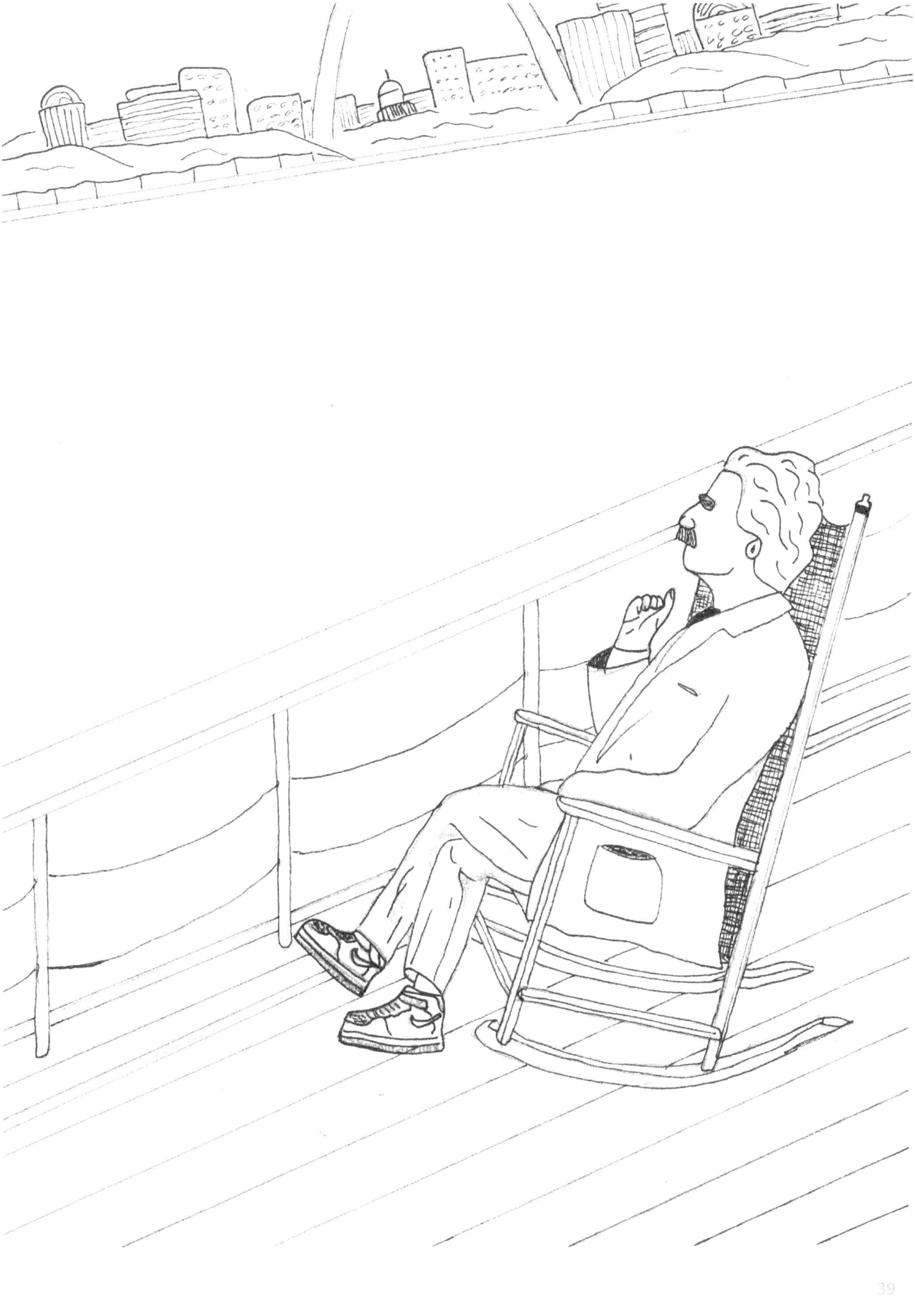

"Sweets of the Show Me State"

Kaycee Lynn Belairs
Senior 2021

Ms. Cheryl Church
Carthage High School
Carthage, Missouri

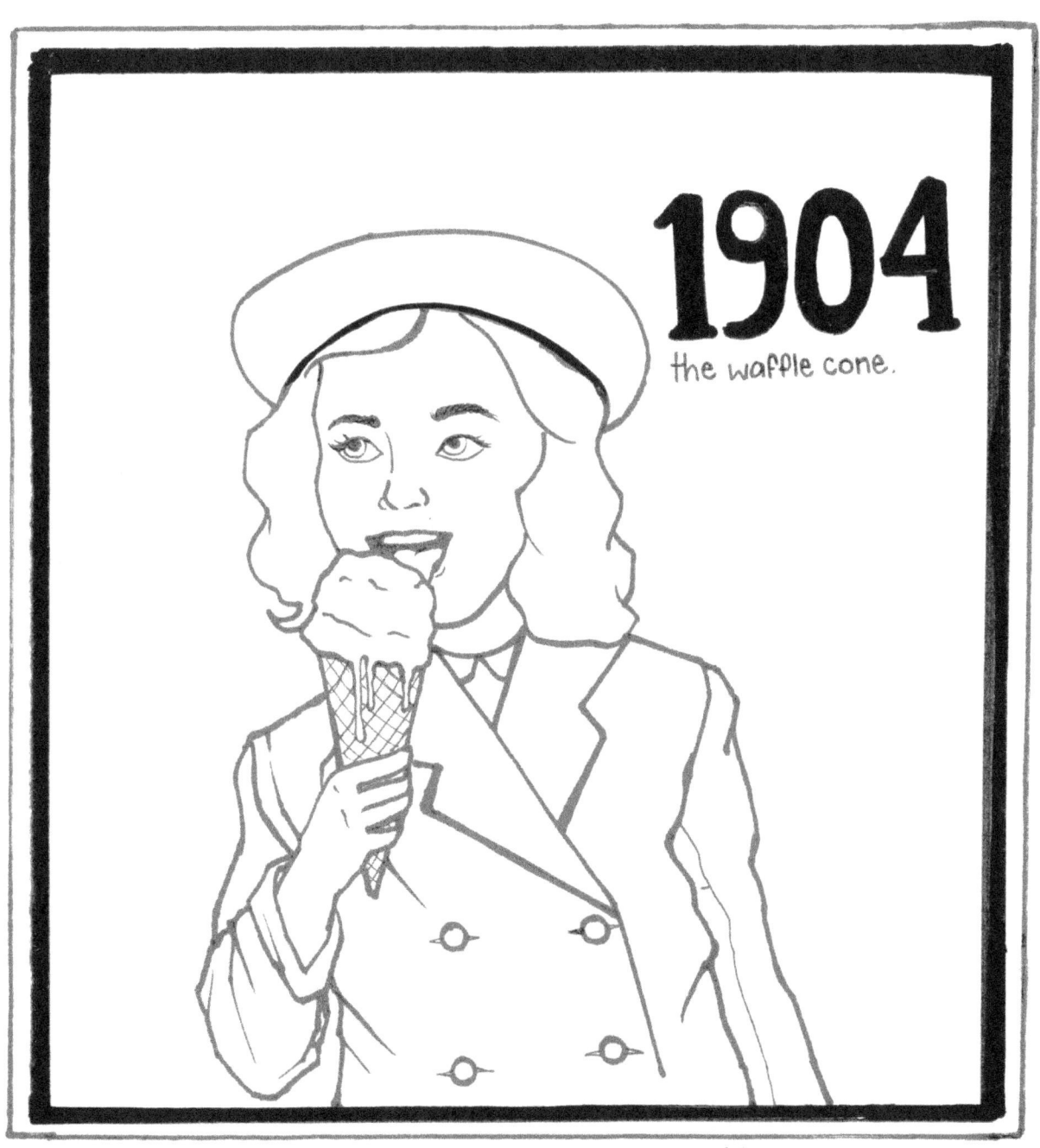

"Conversation"

Gabriel Wilson
Senior

When talking about states, state symbols come to mind. However the majority would likely be overused for this project, yet while searching I didn't see out state flag. After noticing this, I tried to find an idea that would be fun and interesting to draw that incorporated this idea. The idea of the bears in the flag having a conversation came soon after. They need to be talking about something, but since bears don't know English Gibberish was the next best option.

Teacher: Cheryl Church
Carthage High School, Carthage, Missouri

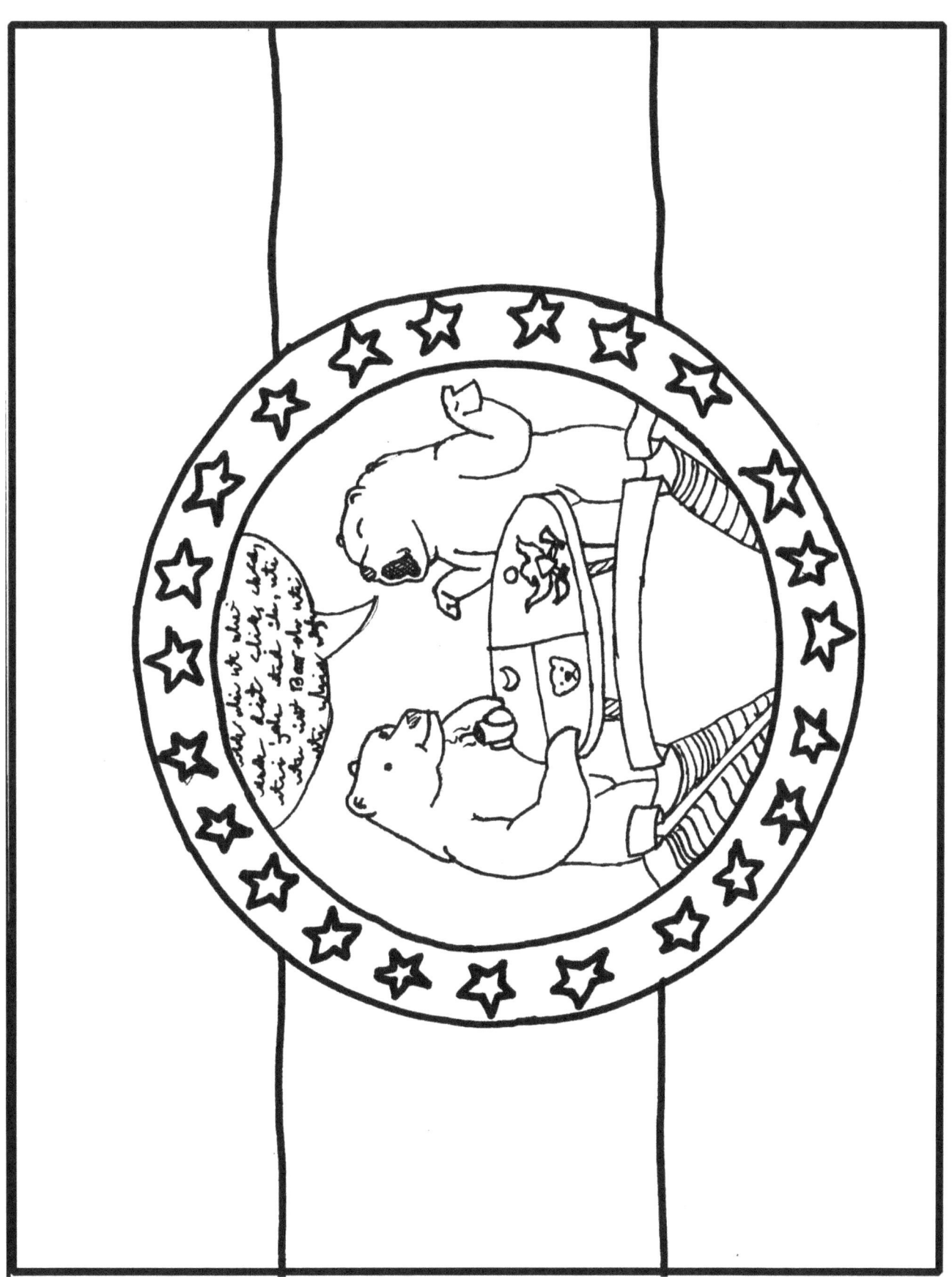

"66 Drive-in Theatre"

Vanessa Marquez
Senior 2021

This drawing shows the 66 Drive-In theatre which is a national historical event district located in my hometown, Carthage, Missouri. It is a part of town to go watch movies outside under the stars and leave with a unforgettable feeling. It brings more excitement to movies with the big screen and the amazing loudspeakers they carry.

Ms. Cheryl Church
Carthage High School
Carthage, Missouri

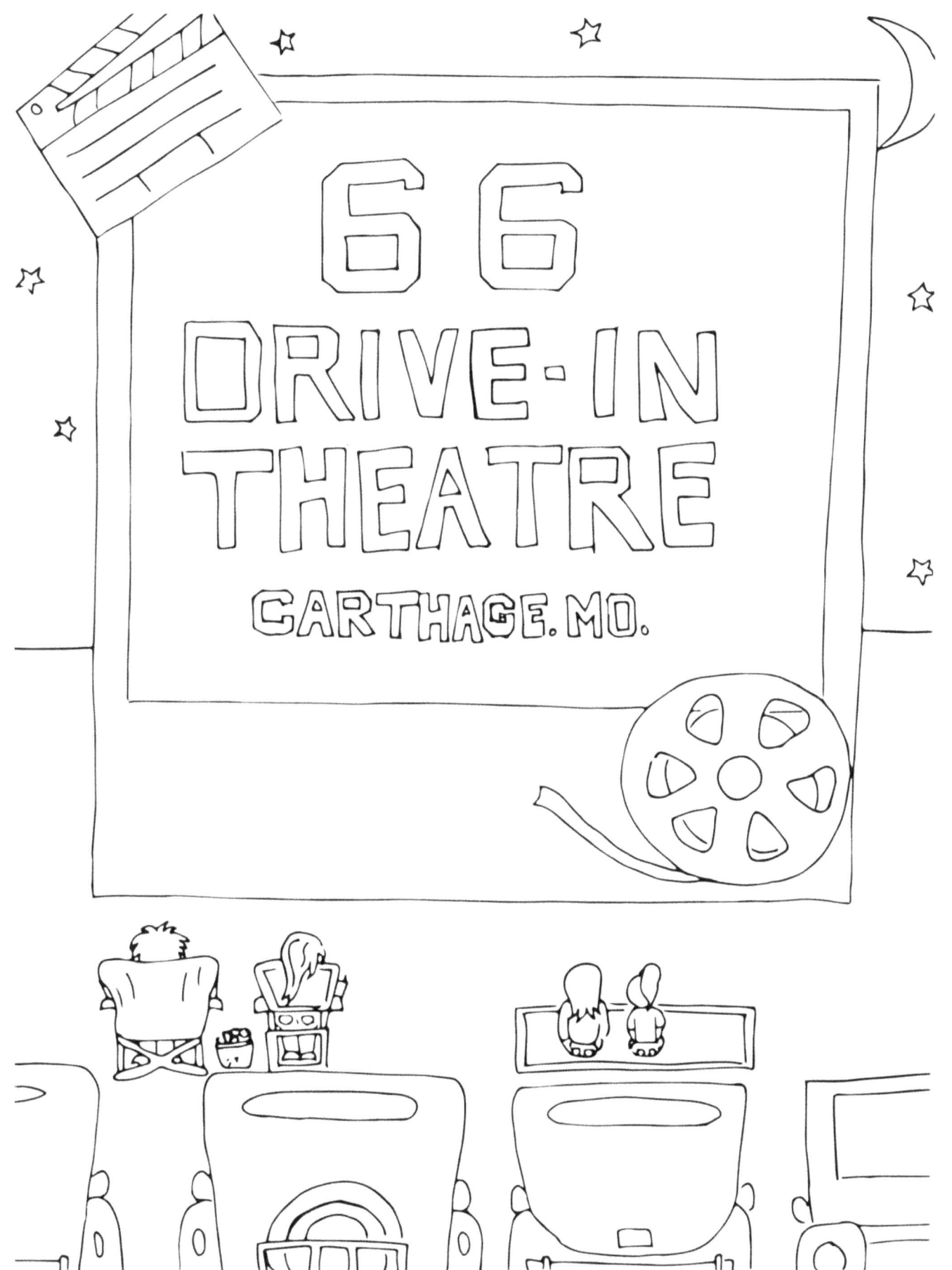

"Nelson-Atkins Museum of Art"

Jade Young
Freshman

Formerly William Rockhill Nelson Gallery of Art and Mary Atkins Museum of Fine Arts, the Nelson-Atkins ranks among the 10 largest in the United States. Opened in 1933, the Nelson-Atkins Museum of Art has more than 30,000 works of art.

Four 18-foot-tall badminton shuttlecocks lie scattered about the lawn across the expansive grounds of the Nelson – Atkins.   Looking like the remains of a giant's game of badminton, the displays were commissioned with funds gifted the museum from the Sosland family.

The works were created by the husband-and-wife team of Claes Oldenburg and Coosje Van Bruggen. Constructed of aluminum and fiberglass pieces taken over a five-day period in July 1994 for installation, the shuttlecocks were inspired by a painting in the museum by Frederic Remington that featured Native Americans wearing feathered headdresses coupled with a satellite image of the museum grounds that resembled a grassy ball court.

Teacher: Stacie Baldwin
Sparta High School
Sparta MO

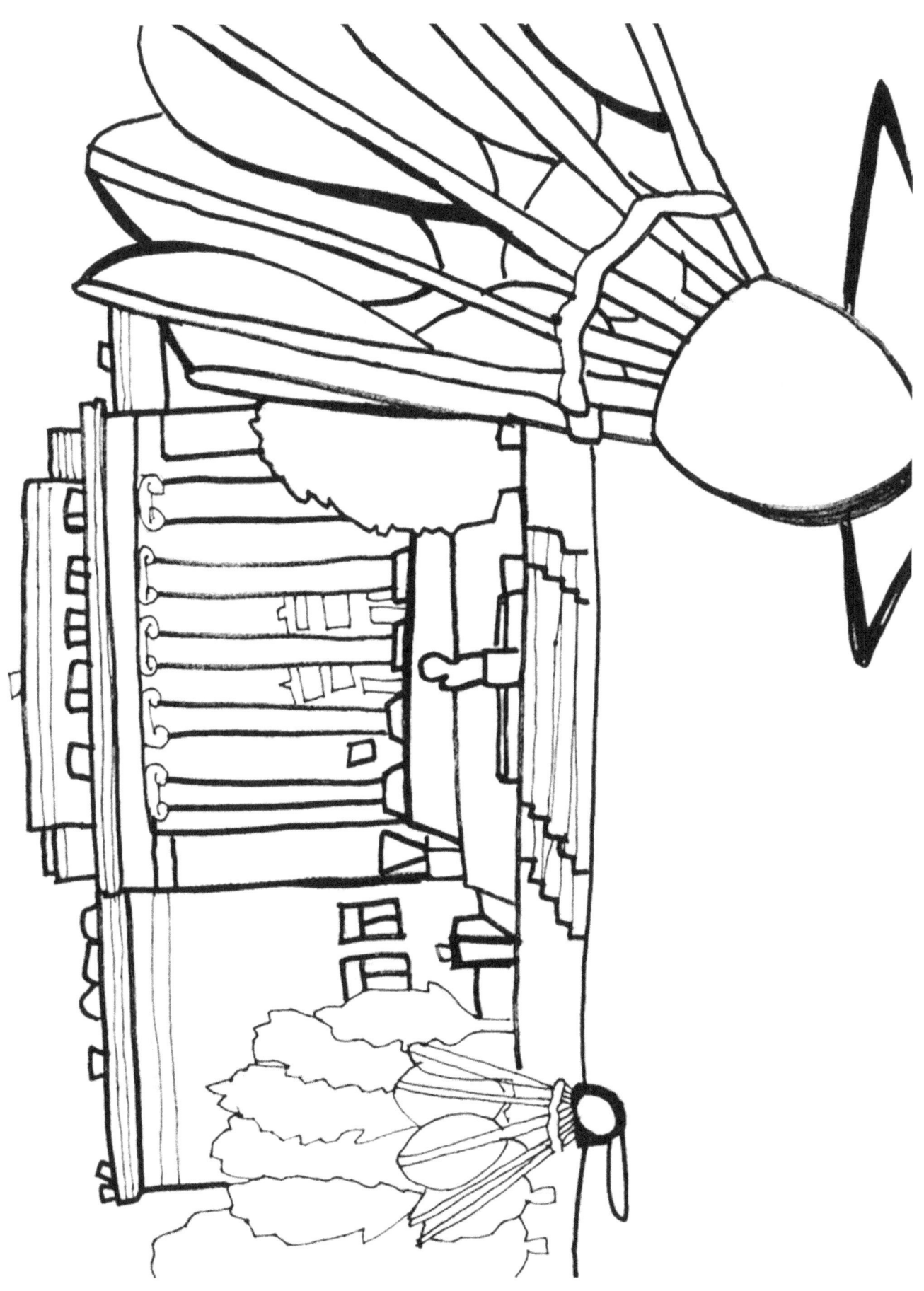

"The Frisco Silver Dollar Line Steam Train"

Kassidy Watts
Senior

The Frisco Silver Dollar Line is a 2 foot (610 mm)narrow-gauge heritage railroad and amusement part attraction located in the Silver Dollar City amusement park in Branson, Missouri. The railroad opened in 1962, making it one of the oldest operating rides at Silver Dollar City. It is themed after American railways in the 1800s. The ride includes an 1800s themed train depot, a water tower, a trestle overpass bridge, a train wreck scene, a staged train robbery, a tunnel, a rectangular shaped roundhouse and an at-grade railroad crossing. It consists of a total of seven steam locomotives, with five of them in operating condition. In 2022, the railroad will be celebrating its 60th anniversary in operation.

Teacher Name
Stacie Baldwin
Sparta High School, Sparta MO

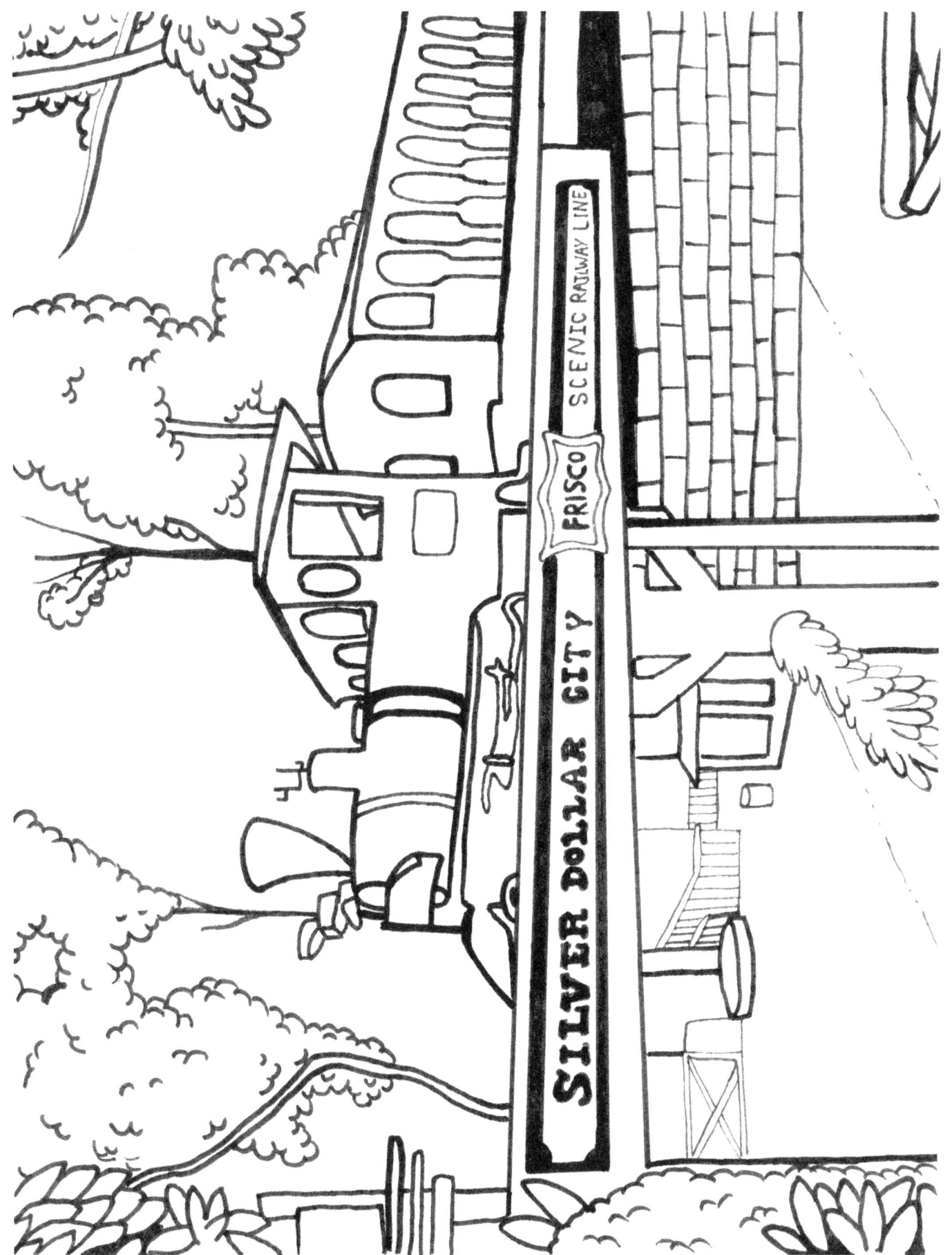

"Old Route 66"

Kullen Myers
Senior

Artist statement:
Although I don't know much about the famous Route 66 that goes
through the heart of Missouri, I have seen signs and know that some nostalgia
is attached to it. It seems that this two lane, windy road is more than a historic
highway, but it represents a life style from the past which is cool to celebrate.
The circles represent the people affected by the road, communities both big
and small, connected in some way- namely by this highway

Teacher: Tana Kettner
Salem High School
Salem, Missouri

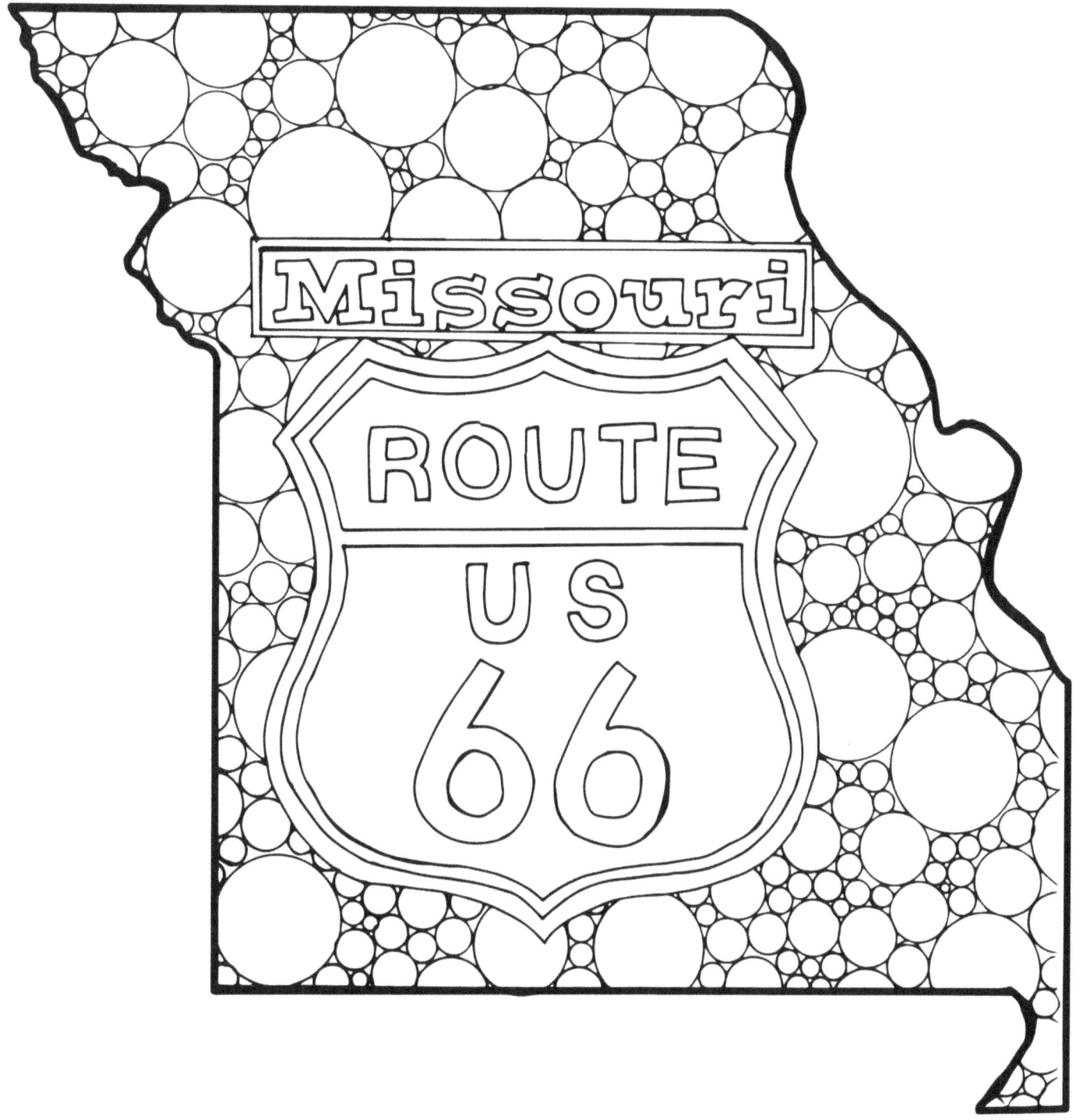

"The Quad"

Crystal Elliott
Senior

Artist statement
A view of The Quad on the University of Missouri-
Columbia campus.

Teacher: Stacie Baldwin
Sparta High School, Sparta MO

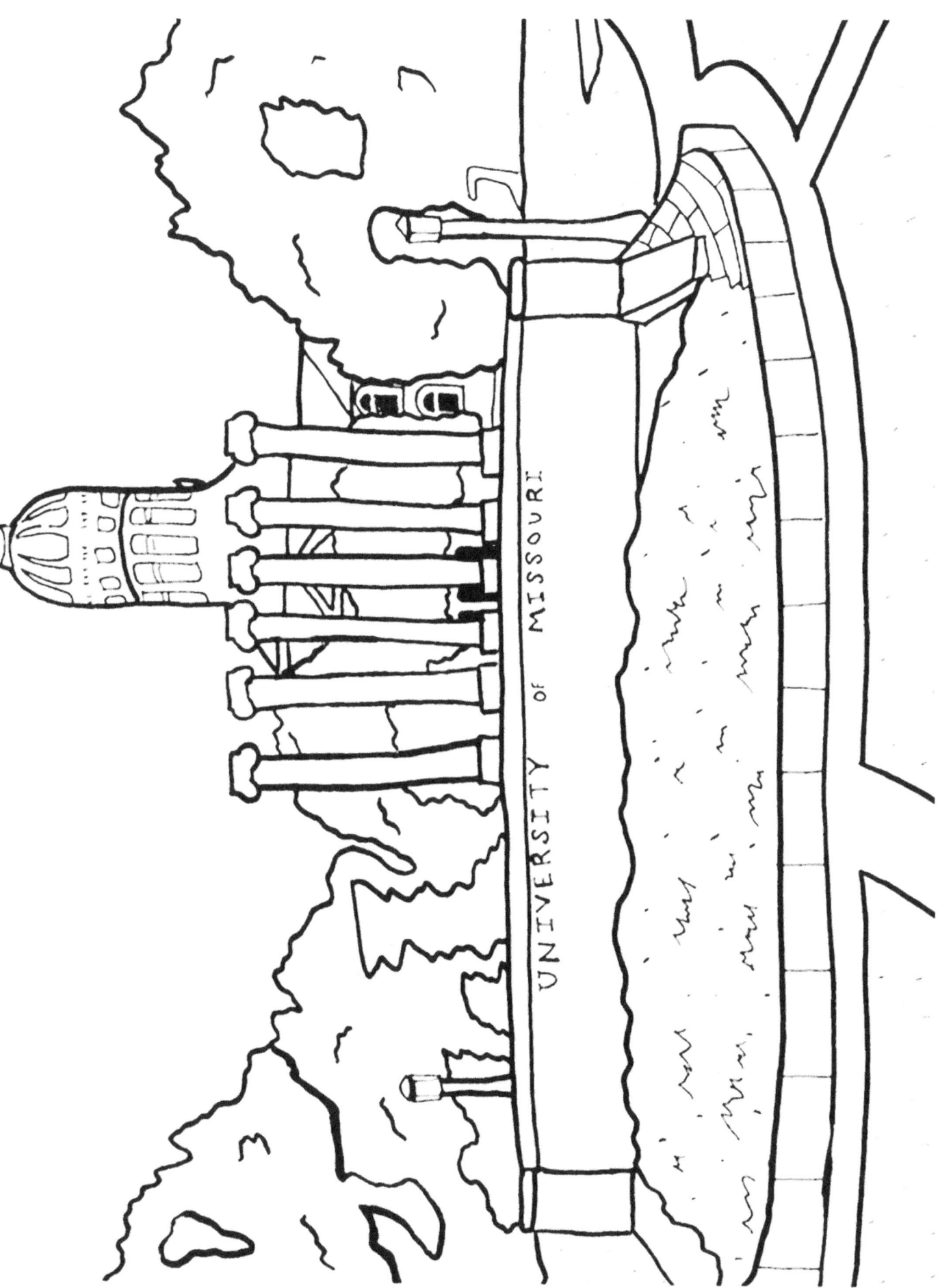

"Sweet Missouri Memory"

Kaitlynn Masterson

My inspiration for my artwork was when I was out strolling the park with my late grandmother. I saw a beautiful bluebird land on a dogwood branch that had just started to sprout the gorgeous pink and white flowers that the dogwood is known for. My depiction of this memory shows Missouri's state bird, the Eastern Bluebird, resting on the Missouri's state tree, the Flowering Dogwood, after a long flight around the town.

Teacher: Whitney Smith
New Madrid County Central

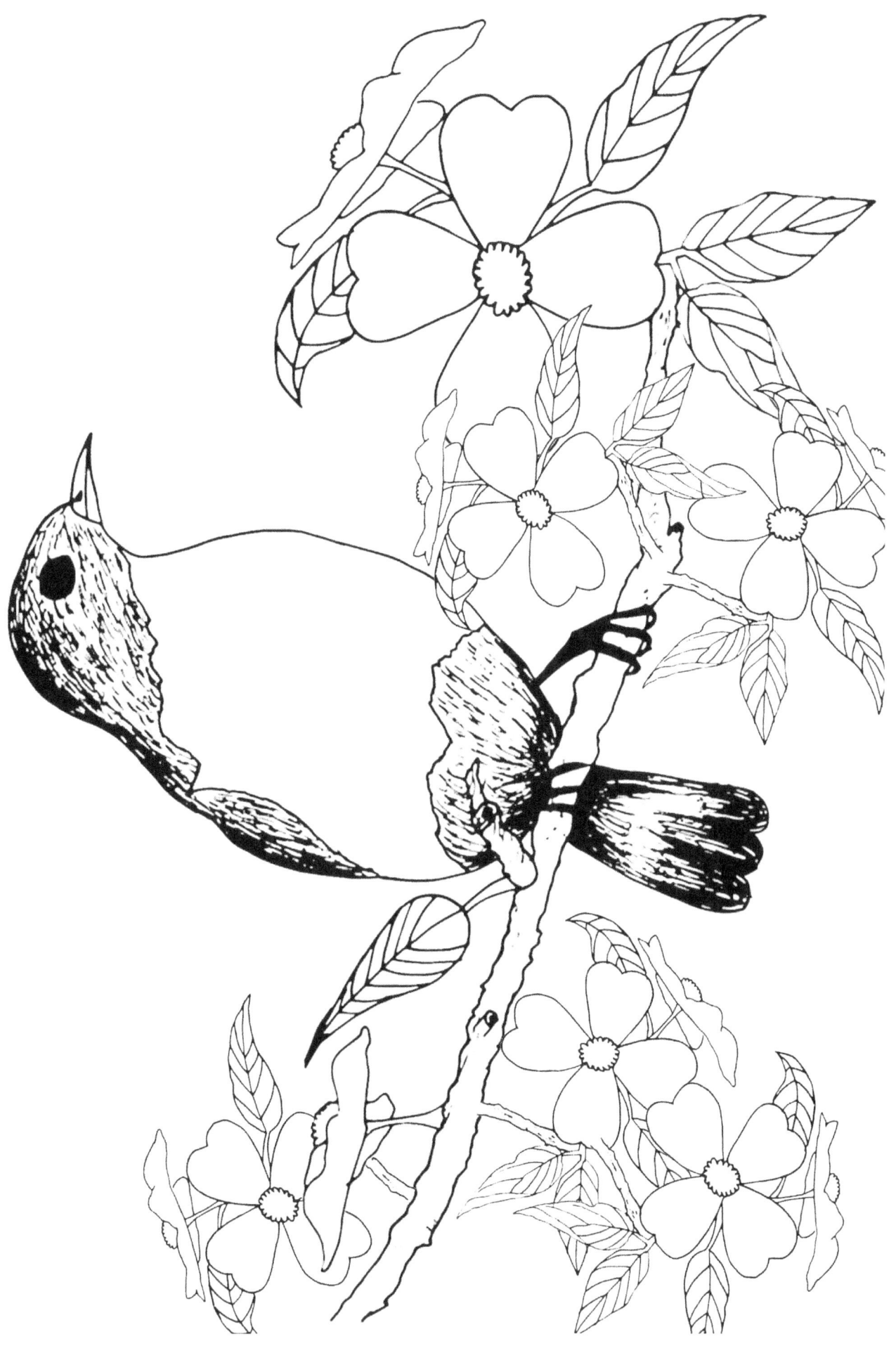

"The Missouri Tree"

Mary Spraggs

My inspiration for this artwork was the state tree witch is flowering dogwood. I wanted to keep the artwork simple and easy to color. I wrote on the artwork "the Missouri tree" in the corner of the page so that anyone coloring would know that it is a branch of the tree.

Teacher: Whitney Smith
New Madrid County Central
New Madrid, Missouri

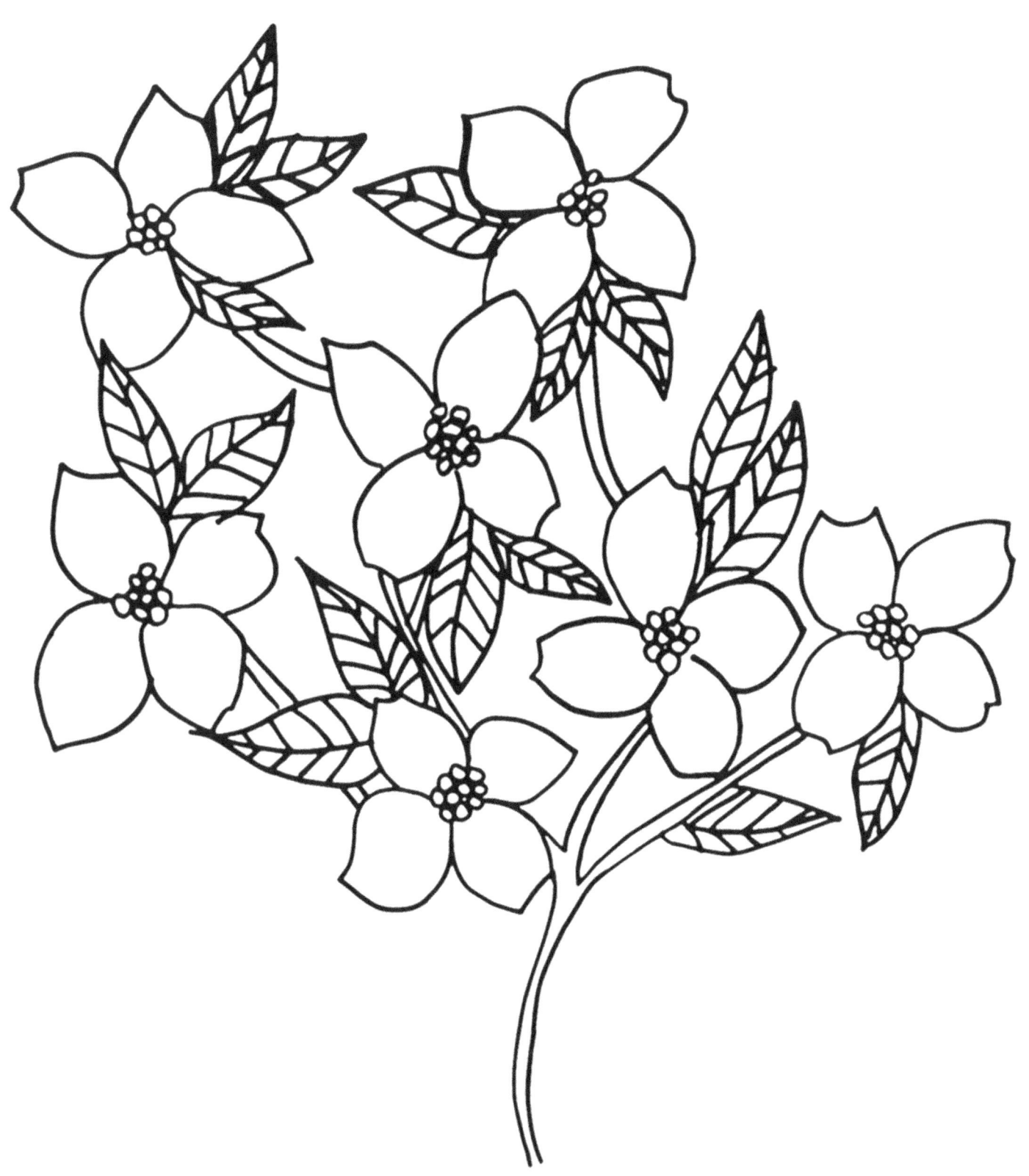

"Show Me The Beauty"

Hailie Edwards

I began thinking about the way to best represent Missouri. Since this artwork was for a coloring book I felt it was best to keep clean lines and the design simplistic so I decided to only draw the states outline. I then drew flowers surrounding the state and wrote our state motto "the show me state" in the middle. I felt the state motto would be a good addition to the piece to add some final touches and add more information about our state.

Teacher: Whitney Smith
New Madrid County Central
New Madrid, Missouri

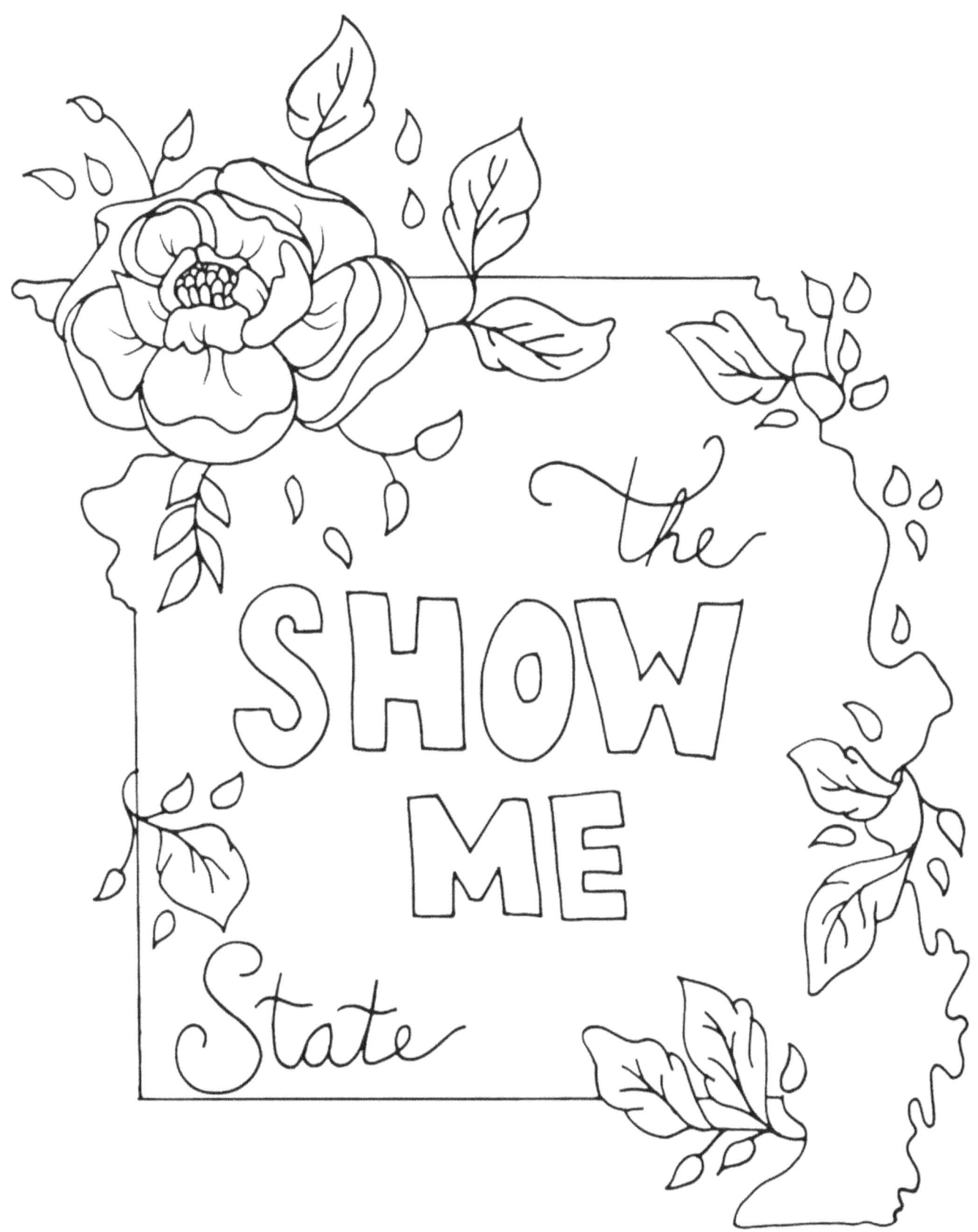

the SHOW ME State

"The Boot-heel"

Josh Phillips

My artwork is an image of Missouri with a boot for the boot-heel, where I live. I also wanted to represent the state bird the blue bird. I then added the honeybee, the state insect, with a trail that spells out "Show Me State". I wanted to represent a couple of our state's most precious figures so I researched some of them on the Missouri state page. I wanted to create a simplistic and cartoony artwork so I used animated faces and gave inanimate objects human features.

Teacher: Whitney Smith
New Madrid County Central
New Madrid, Missouri

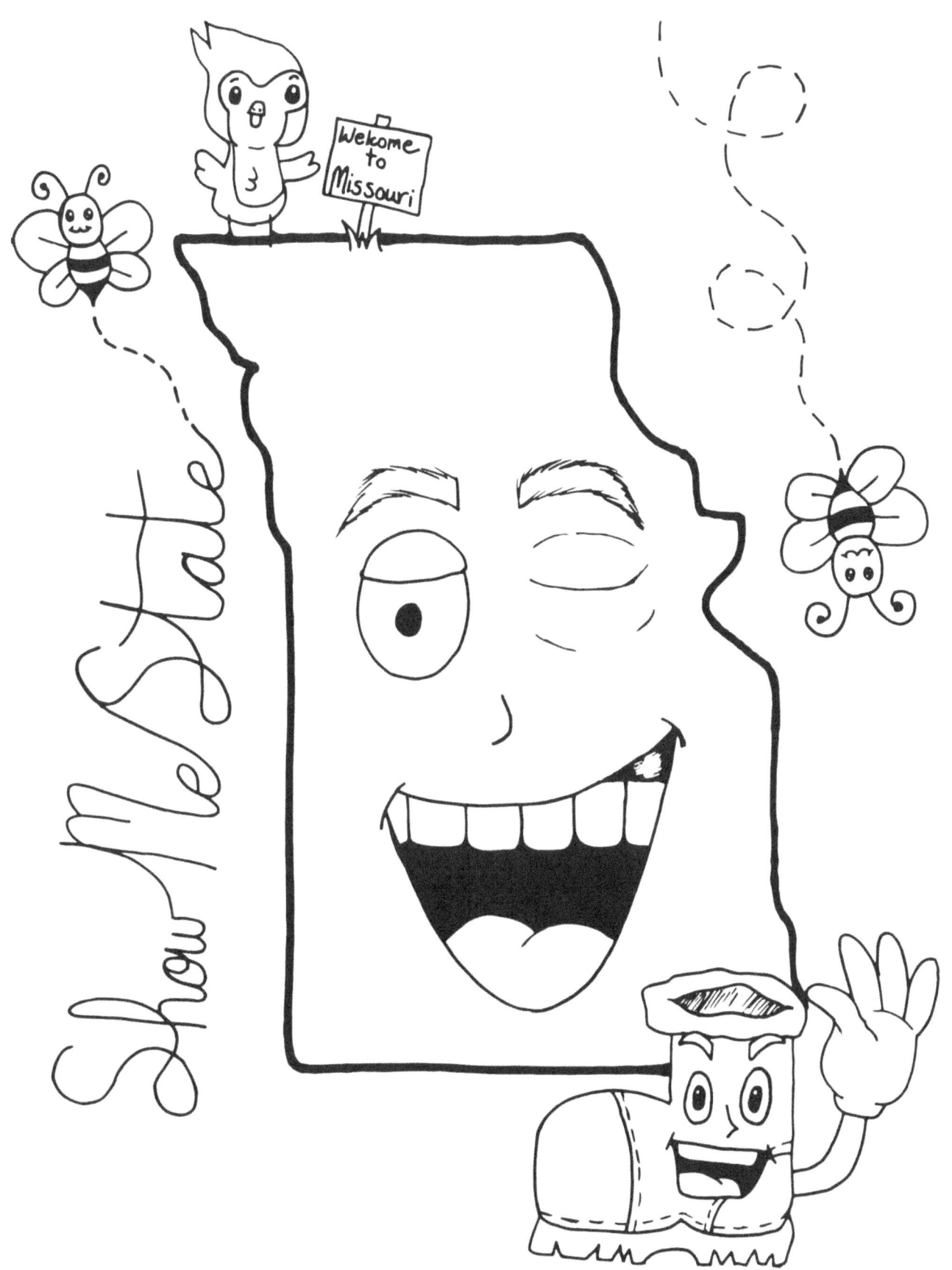

"Edythe Baker"

Melissa Hendrickson
Senior 2020

Edythe A. Baker (August 25, 1899 – August 15, 1971) was an American jazz pianist born in poverty in Girard, Kansas. After her mother died in 1910 Edythe was sent to Kansas City Missouri to live, and attend a convent. There she gained training in piano fundamentals. She later toured with vaudeville troupe in 1918, later moving to New York where she made piano rolls such as ragtime and pop pieces. She worked on Broadway in musicals and performed with Ziegfeld Follies. In 1926 Baker relocated to England where she recorded twenty two pieces. She became a star after appearing in revues in 1927.   Edythe left the music industry after the mid 1930s to marry.

Teacher: Nellie Mitchell
Carl Junction High School
Carl Junction, Missouri

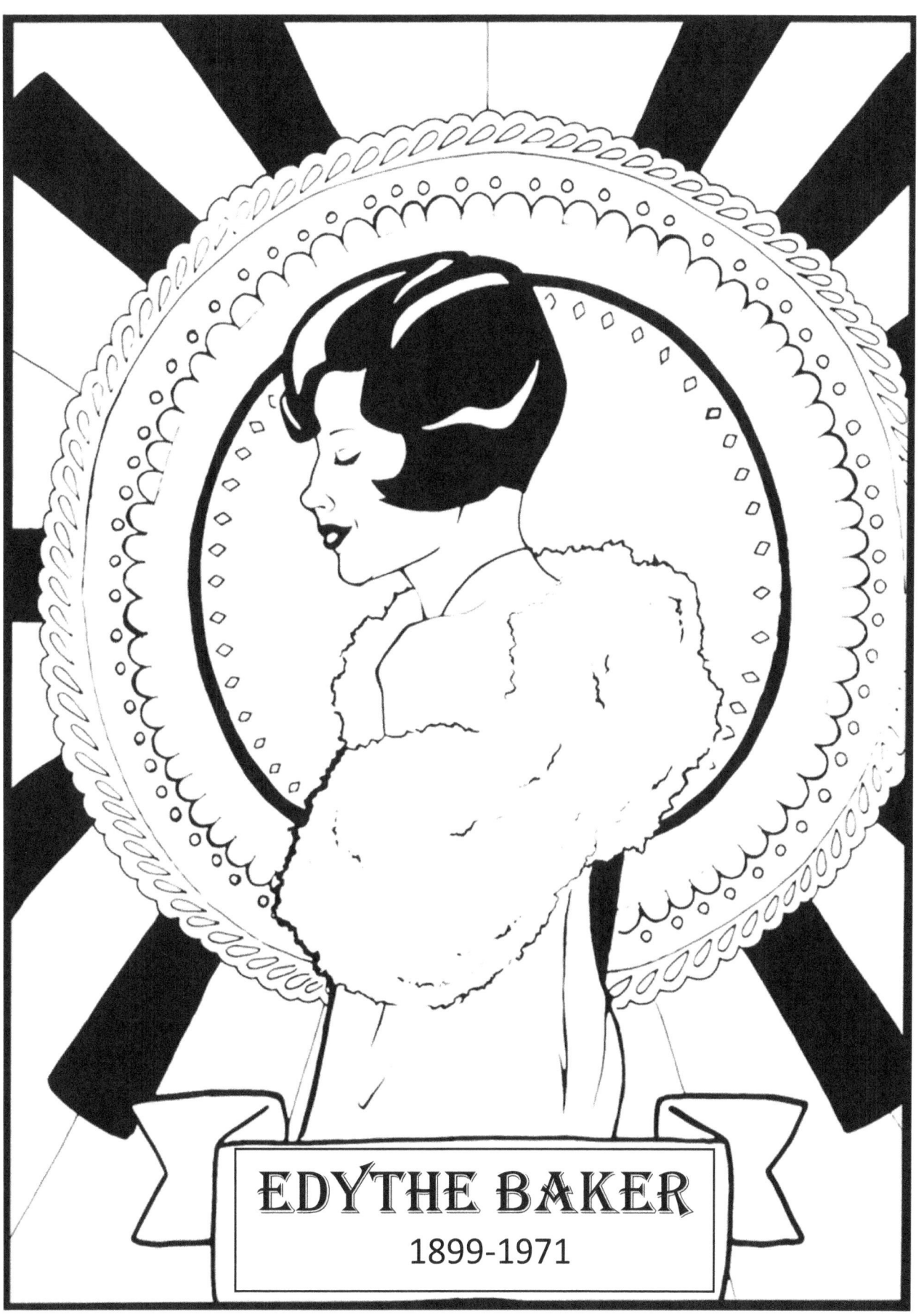

EDYTHE BAKER

1899-1971

"Bugs of Missouri"

Olivea Kittrell
Graduate 2019

Teacher: Nellie Mitchell
Carl Junction High School
Carl Junction, Missouri

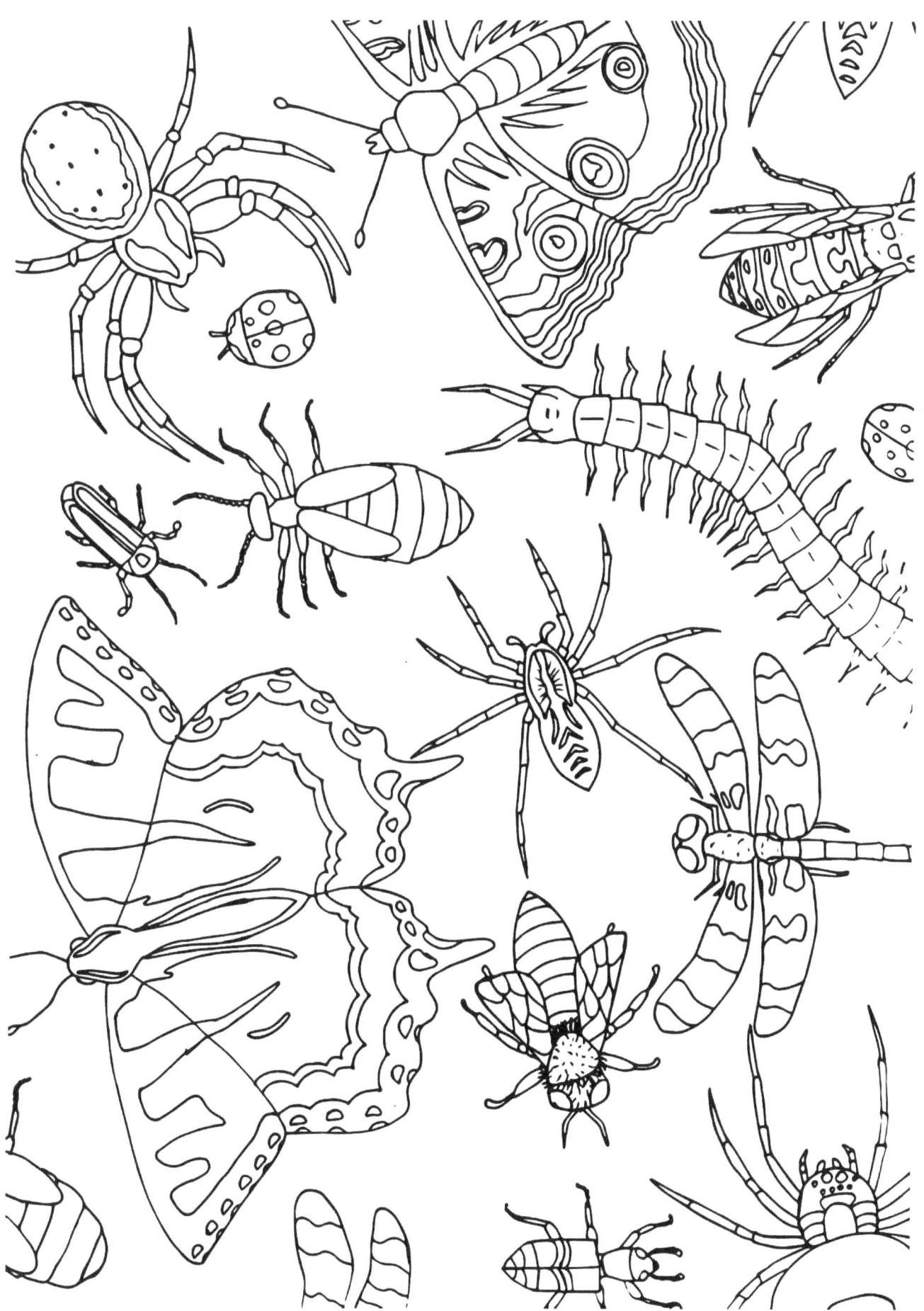

"Missouri Dessert"

Kenzie Smith
Senior 2020

Whether the end of the meal or a simple indulgence, we all like to have something sweet now and then. There's no sweeter state than Missouri.

On Aug. 28, 2008 the "Show Me State" join the ranks of other foodie states with an official dessert, the ice cream cone. On July 10, 2008, Gov. Matt Blunt signed the bill proclaiming the ice cream cone as the official dessert of our "Show Me State".

How did the ice cream cone come about? According to fair legend, two vendors, one who made waffle cakes and one who served ice cream, worked next to one another at The St. Louis State Fair in 1904. The ice cream vendor ran out of dishes to serve his product a vendor suggested they take a pastry and put the ice cream in it. And just like that the state dessert was born.

Teacher: Nellie Mitchell
Carl Junction High School
Carl Junction, Missouri

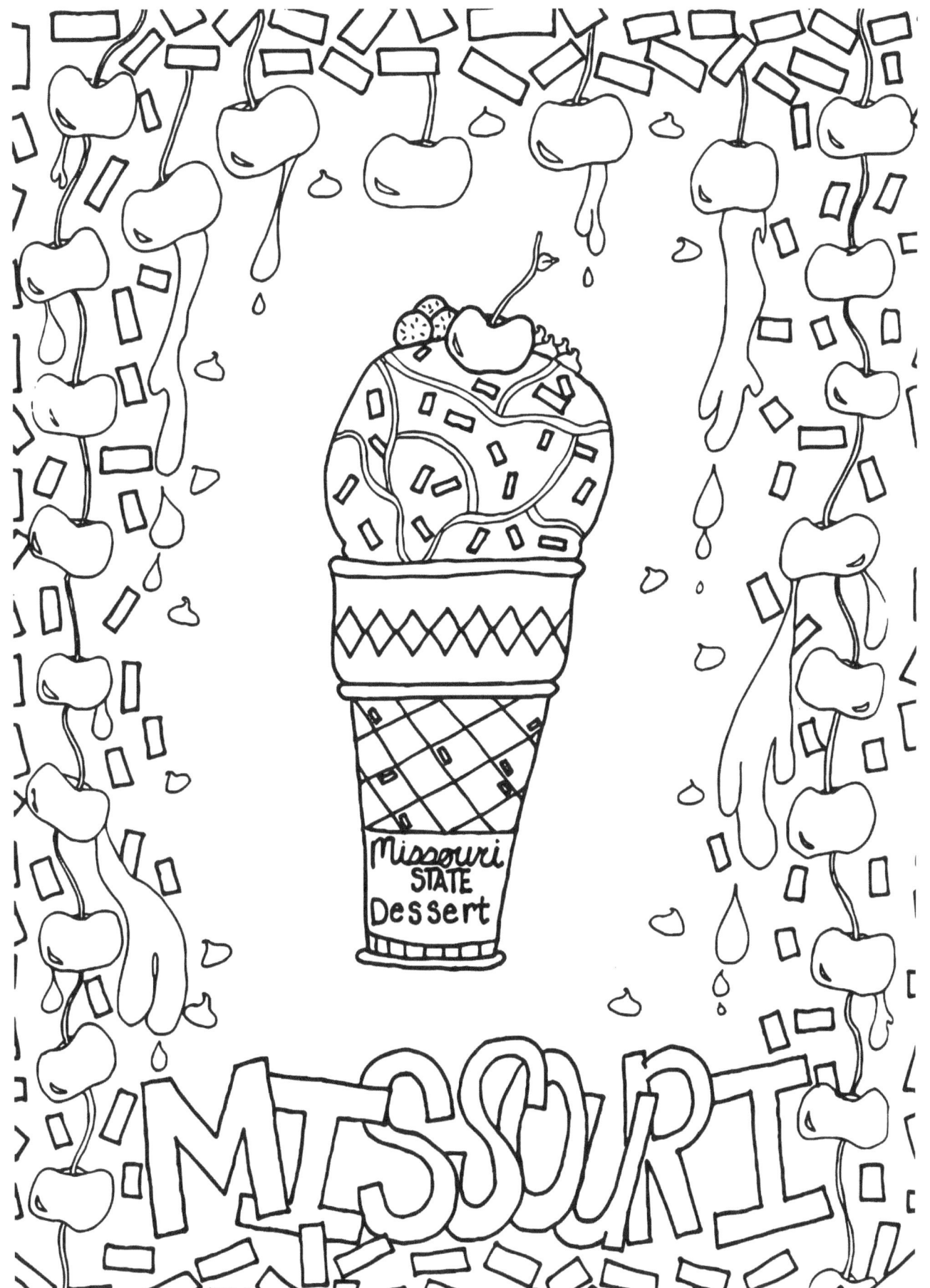

"Missouri Pops"

Anna Kaye Vangilder
Junior

Teacher: Nellie Mitchell
Carl Junction High School
Carl Junction, Missouri

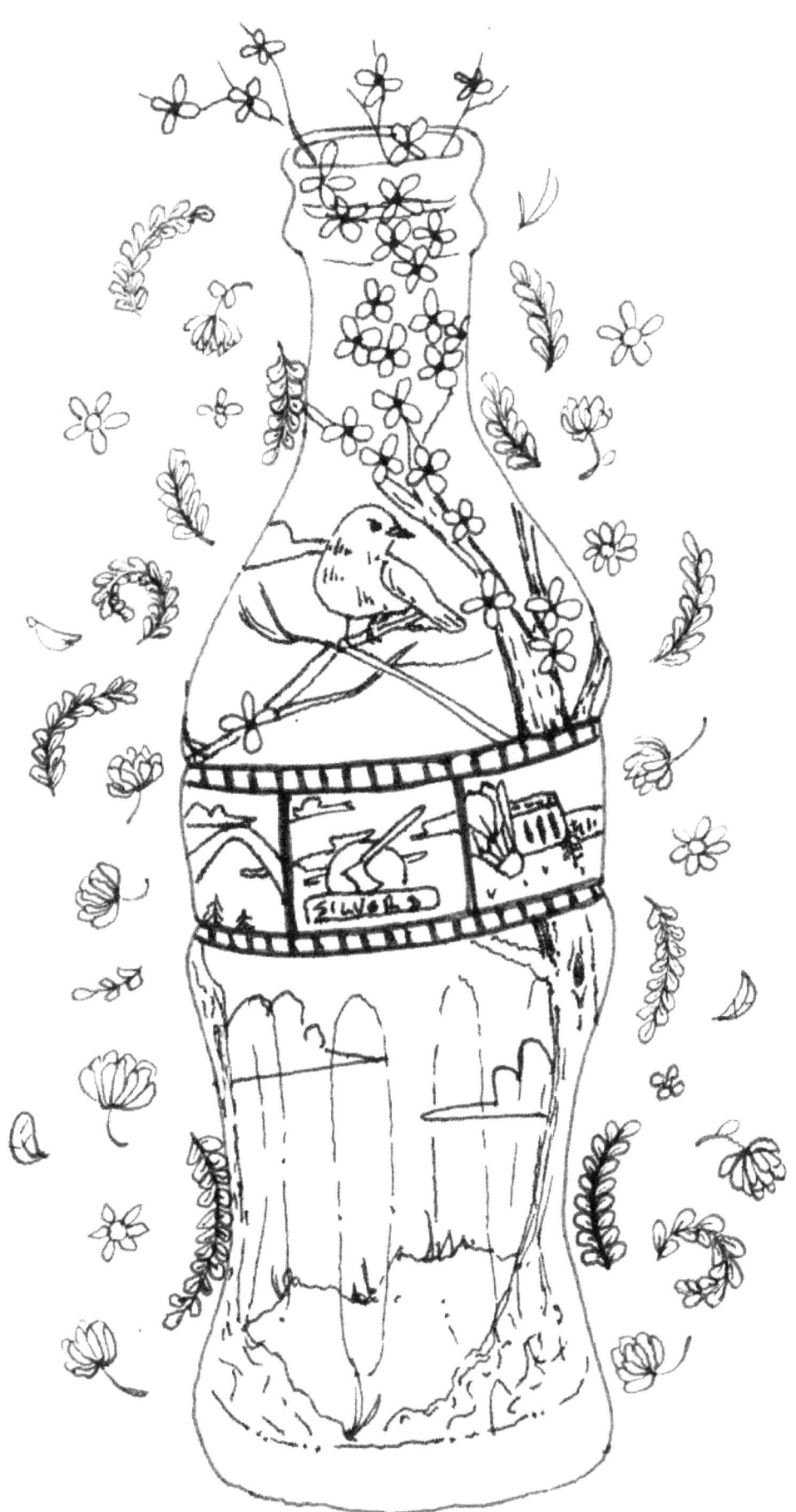

"Kansas City BBQ"

Theresa Rodriguez
Senior 2020

When it comes to barbecue, Kansas City is a regional
style rooted in a history of tradition and, in recent years, eclecticism.
From a willingness to use all forms of meat, to endless variations
on the region's sweet and somewhat spicy tomato-based barbecue
sauce, there's room for diversity among the many establishments.

Teacher: Nellie Mitchell
Carl Junction High School
Carl Junction, Missouri

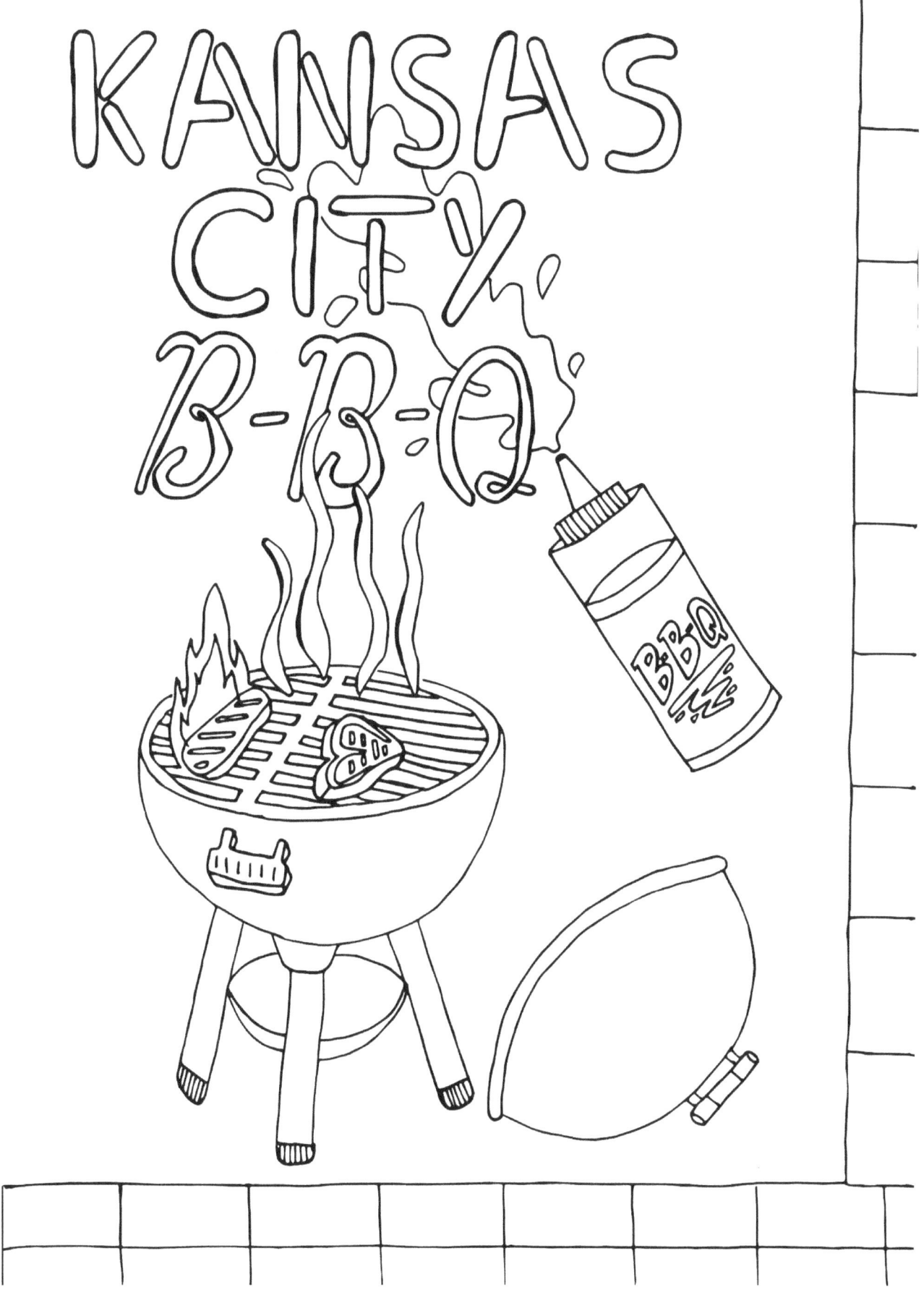

"Birdie of KC"

Maggie Brown
Junior

Teacher: Nellie Mitchell
Carl Junction High School
Carl Junction, Missouri

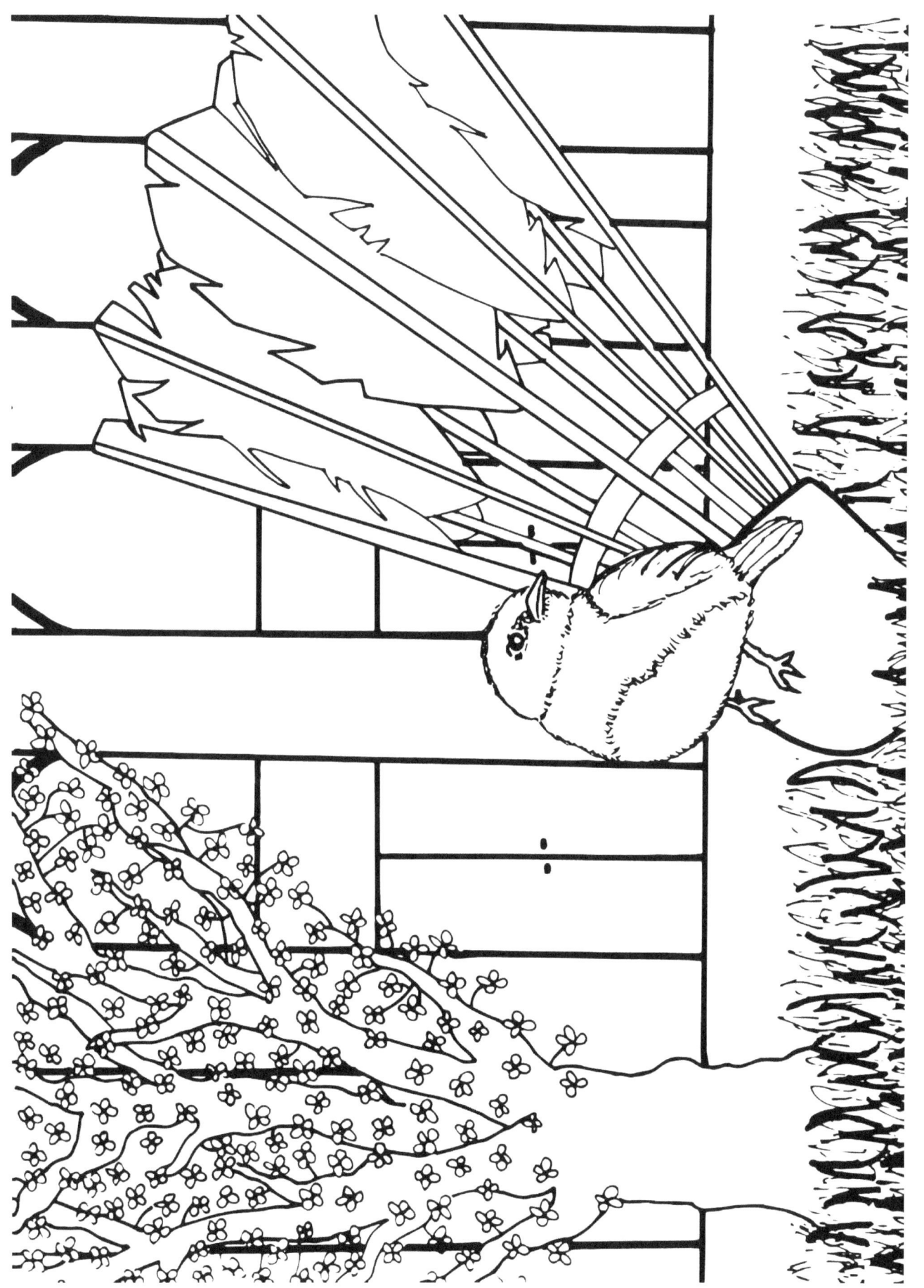

"Elephant Rocks"

Tobey Larson

Teacher: David Mitchell
S.C.O.R.E. Of Nixa Public Schools
Nixa, MO

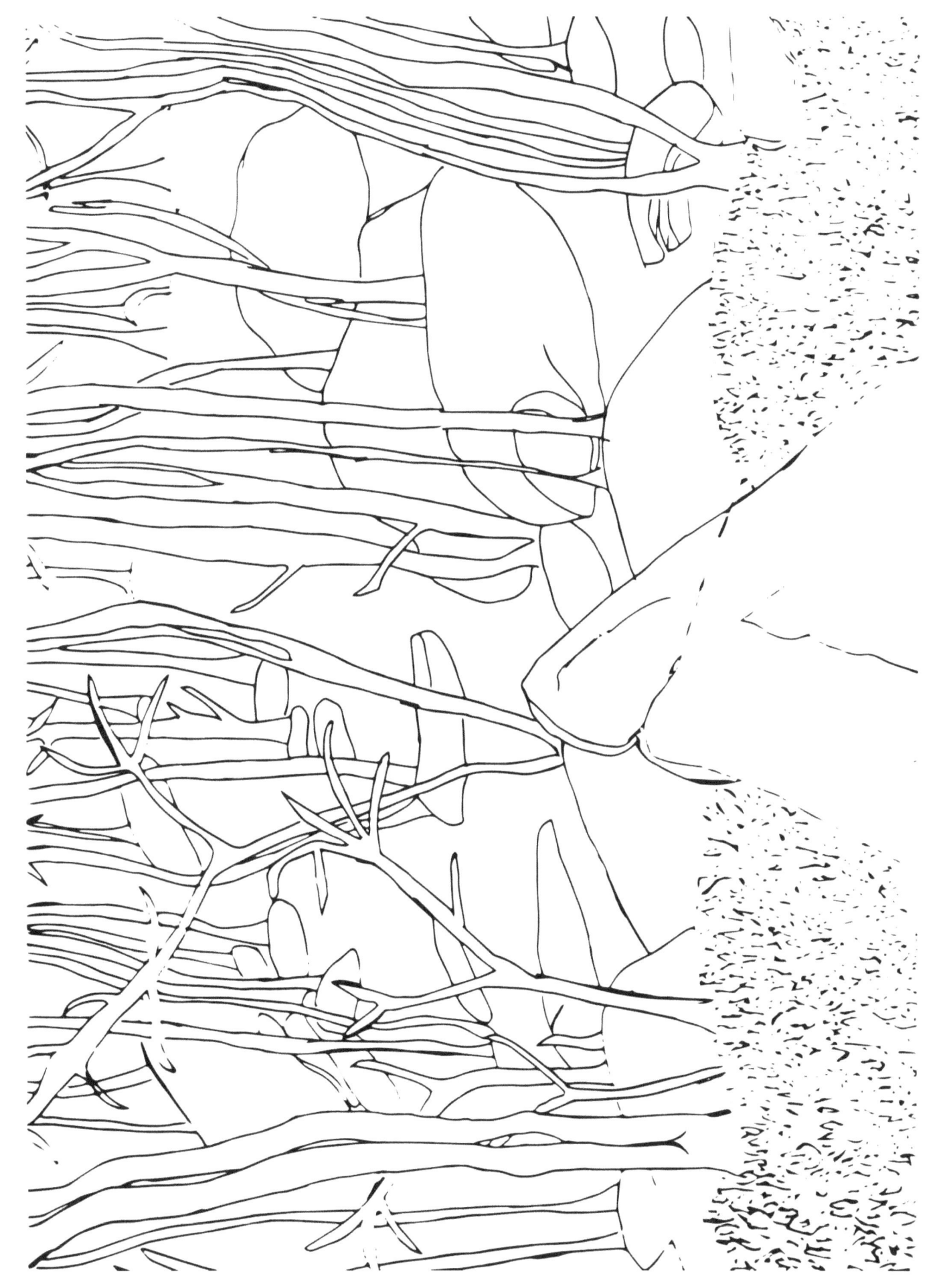

"Fantastic Caverns"

Raven Jacob

The cavern was discovered by John Knox and his hunting dog in 1862. Knox did not want the cave to be exploited by the Union or Confederate governments, so he kept the cave's existence quiet until 1867. Knox put an advertisement in the Springfield paper for someone to explore the cave. On February 27, twelve women belonging to the Springfield Women's Athletic Club explored Fantastic Caverns. These twelve ladies are considered the first explorers of the Ozarks cave. Their names are still visible on the cavern walls today. The cave has had many uses throughout the different owners such as a speakeasy during the Prohibition years and hosted live music concerts during the 1950s and 1960s.

Teacher:
Nixa High School
Nixa, Missouri

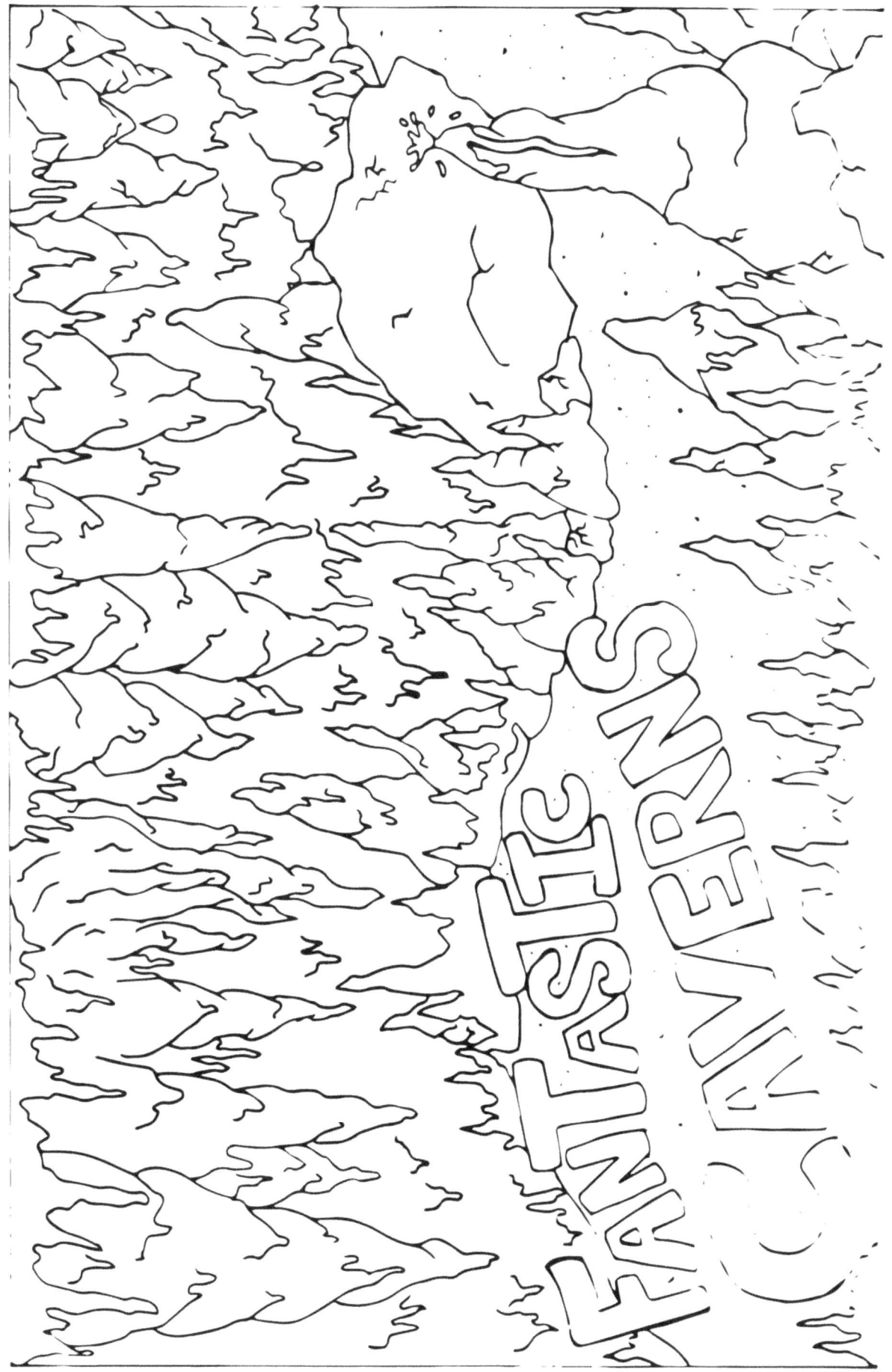

Hypsibema Missouriensis

Lucus Bostic
Senior 2021

Delegated as the Official State Dinosaur of Missouri, the duck-billed dinosaur (Hadrosaur) lived in Missouri about 75 million years ago during the Late Cretaceous period.   The Hypsibema missouriense fossil was discovered in 1942 near the town of Glen Allen, Missouri. The bones were the first known find of dinosaur bones in Missouri.

Teacher Rosemary Ziegler
Truman High School
Truman, Missouri

Hypsibema
Missouriensis

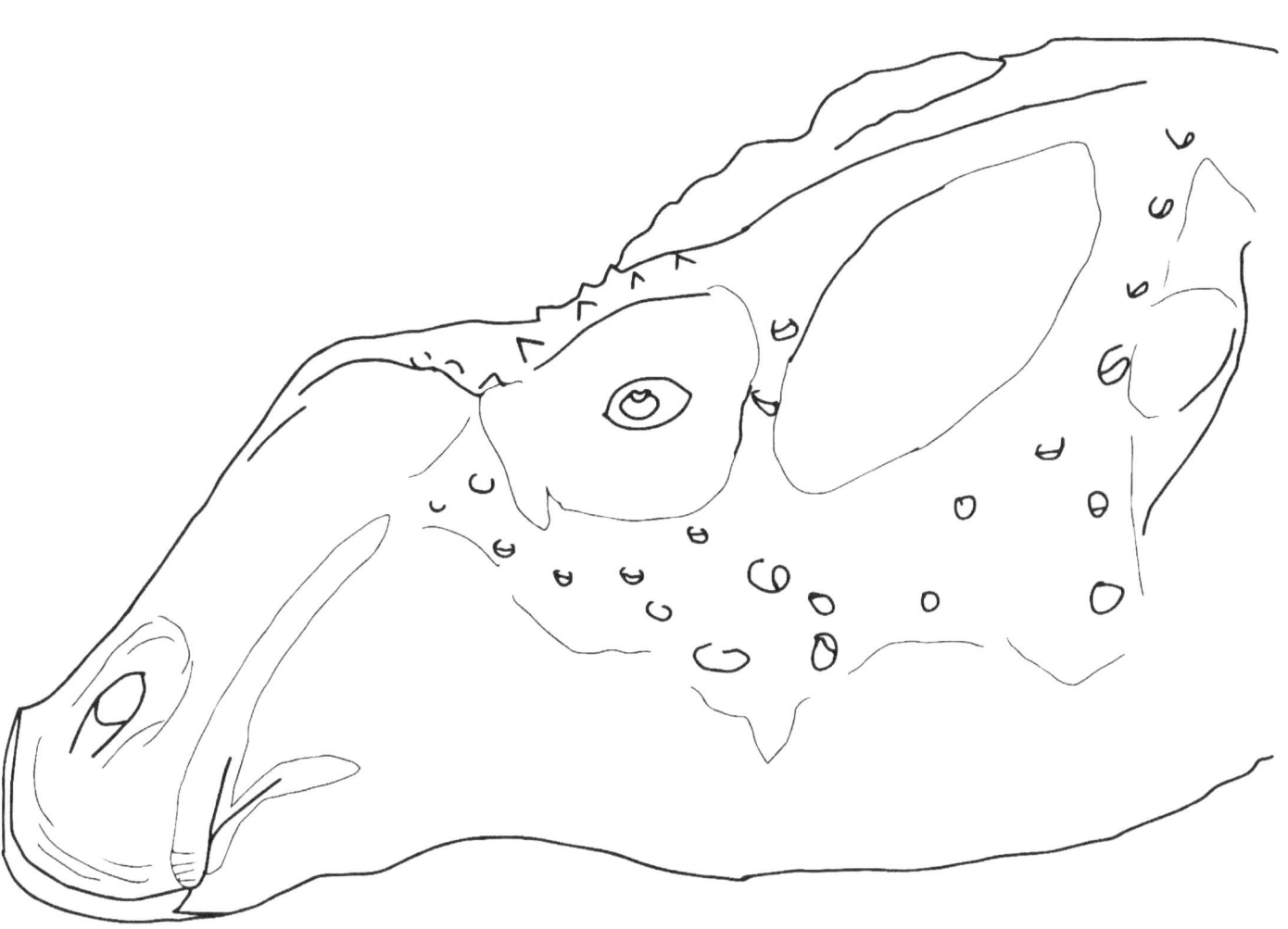

Downtown

Jessica Jenkins
11th

Teacher: **Rosemary Ziegler**
Truman High School
Truman, Missouri

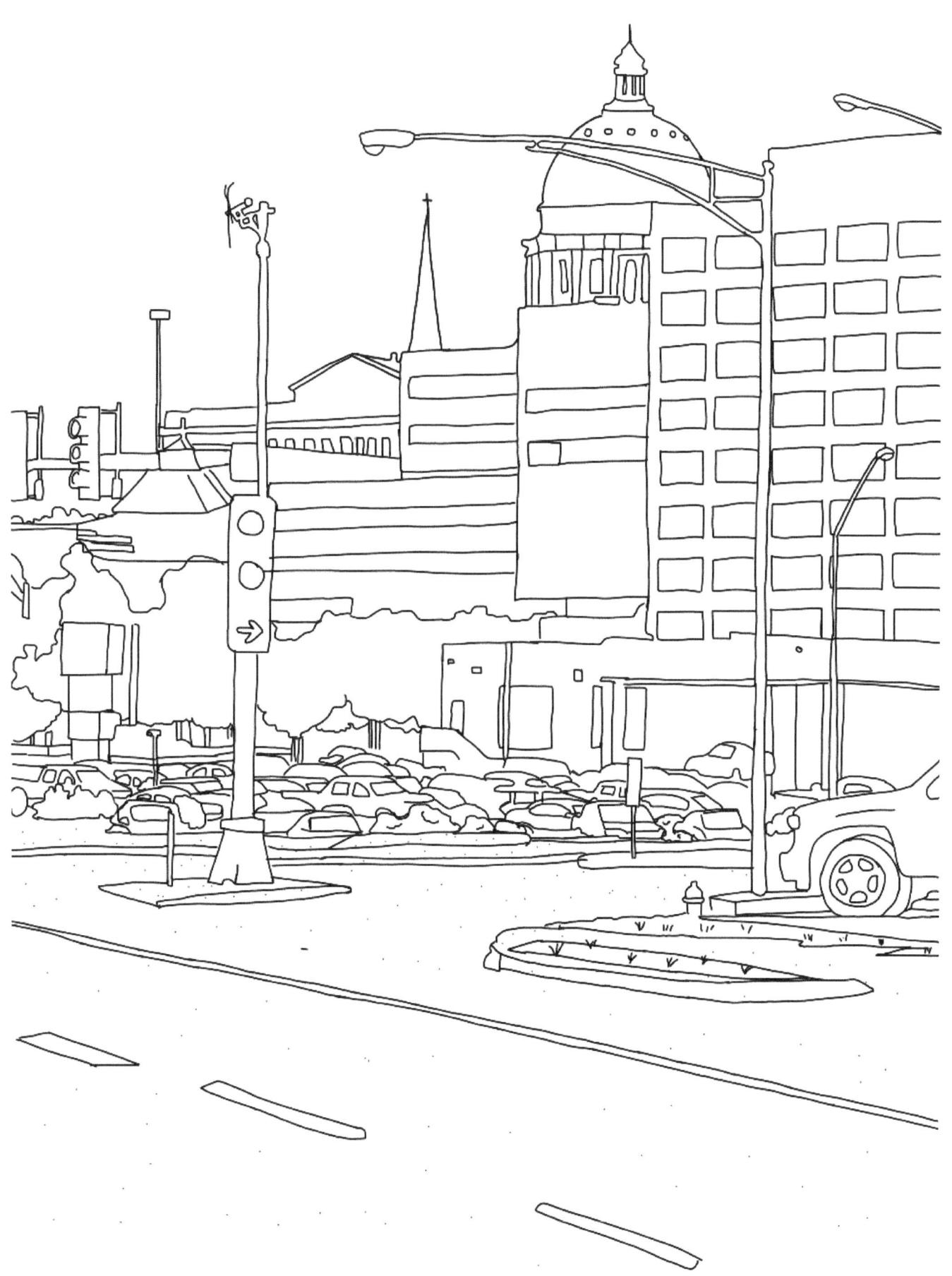

Obelisk

Oliver Elders
11th

Teacher: Rosemary Ziegler
Truman High School
Truman, Missouri

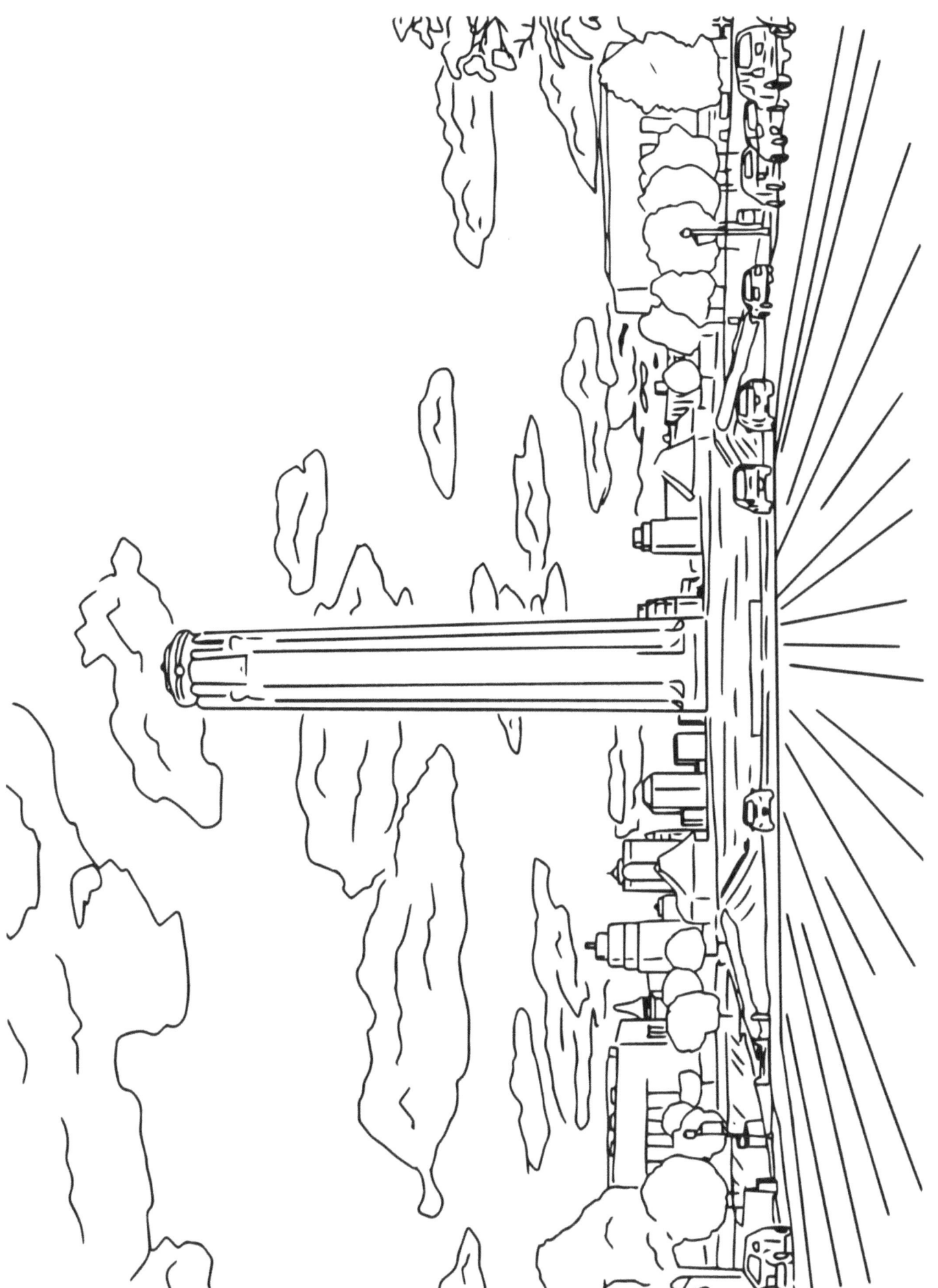

"Missouri Eastern Blue Bird"

Lali Esquivel
12th grade

"I drew this eastern blue bird because it's really beautiful and majestic. The flowers complement the bird and are called Grataegus Punctats which is the state flower".

Teacher: Elizabeth Wallsmith
Monett High School
Monett, Missouri

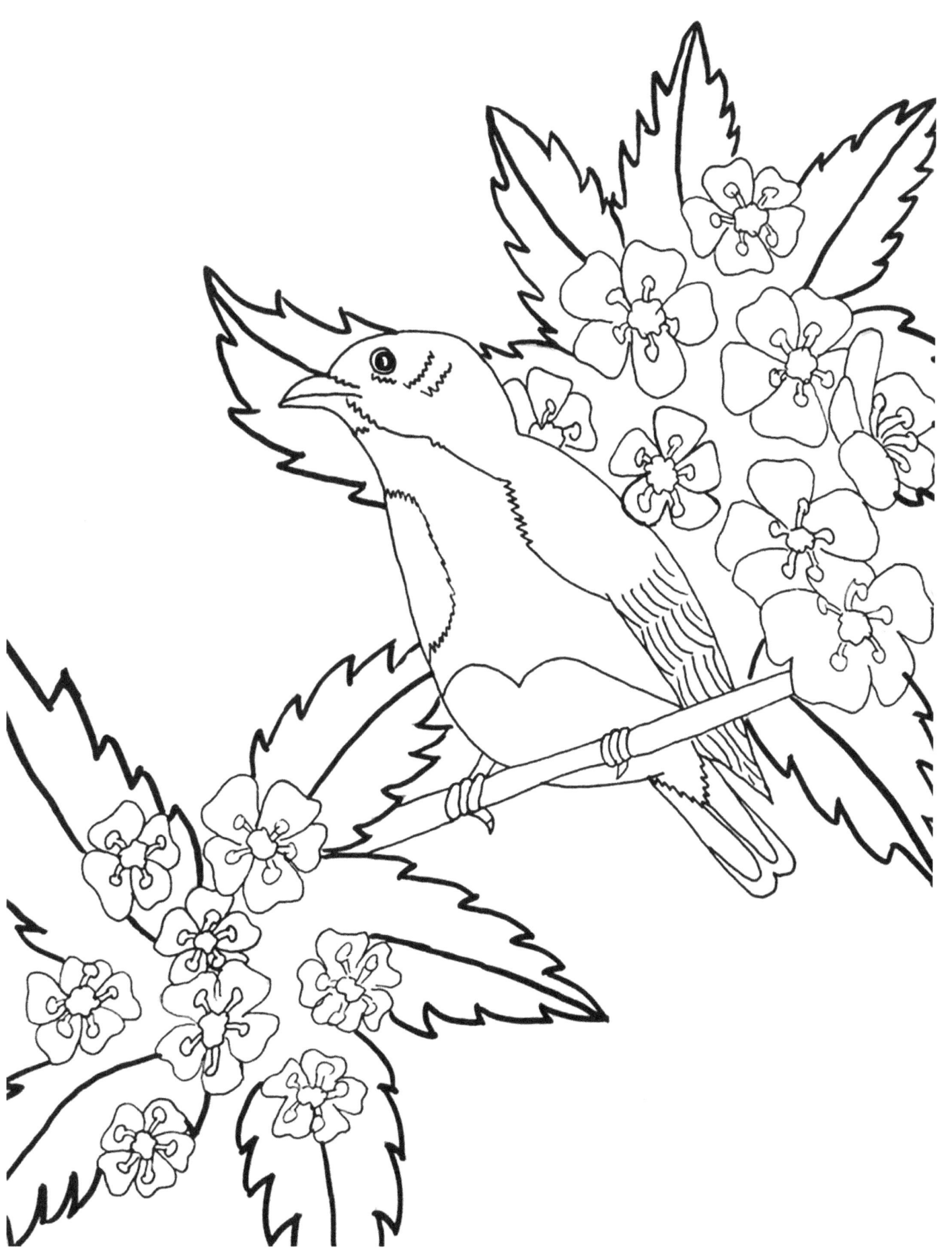

"Missouri State Bird"

Lesilee Jones
Freshman

Teacher: Amy Rushing
Waynesville High School
Waynesville, Missouri

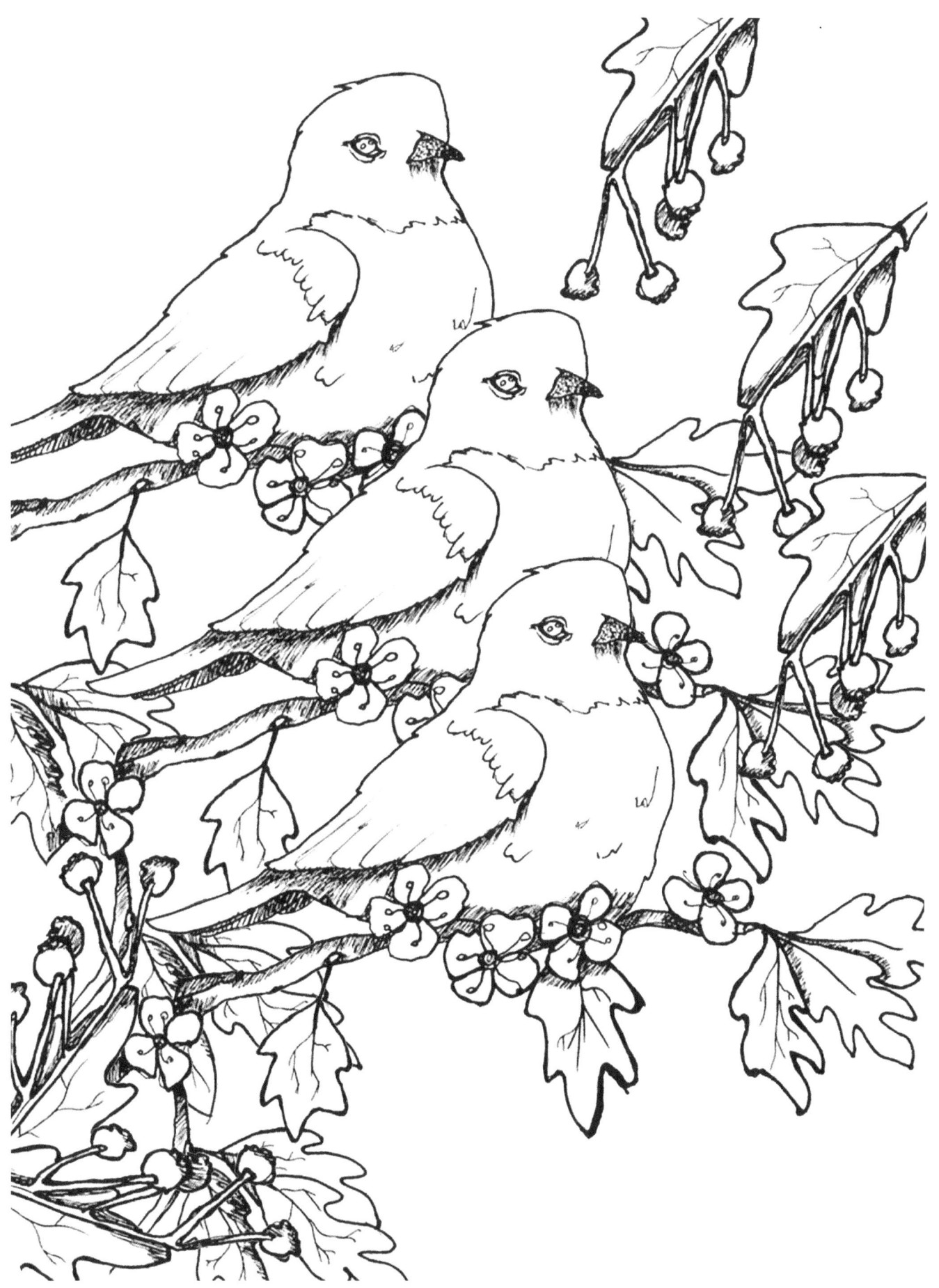

"Missouri Blue Bird"

Tristan Creson

Teacher: Sarah Luttrell
Waynesville High School
Waynesville, Missouri

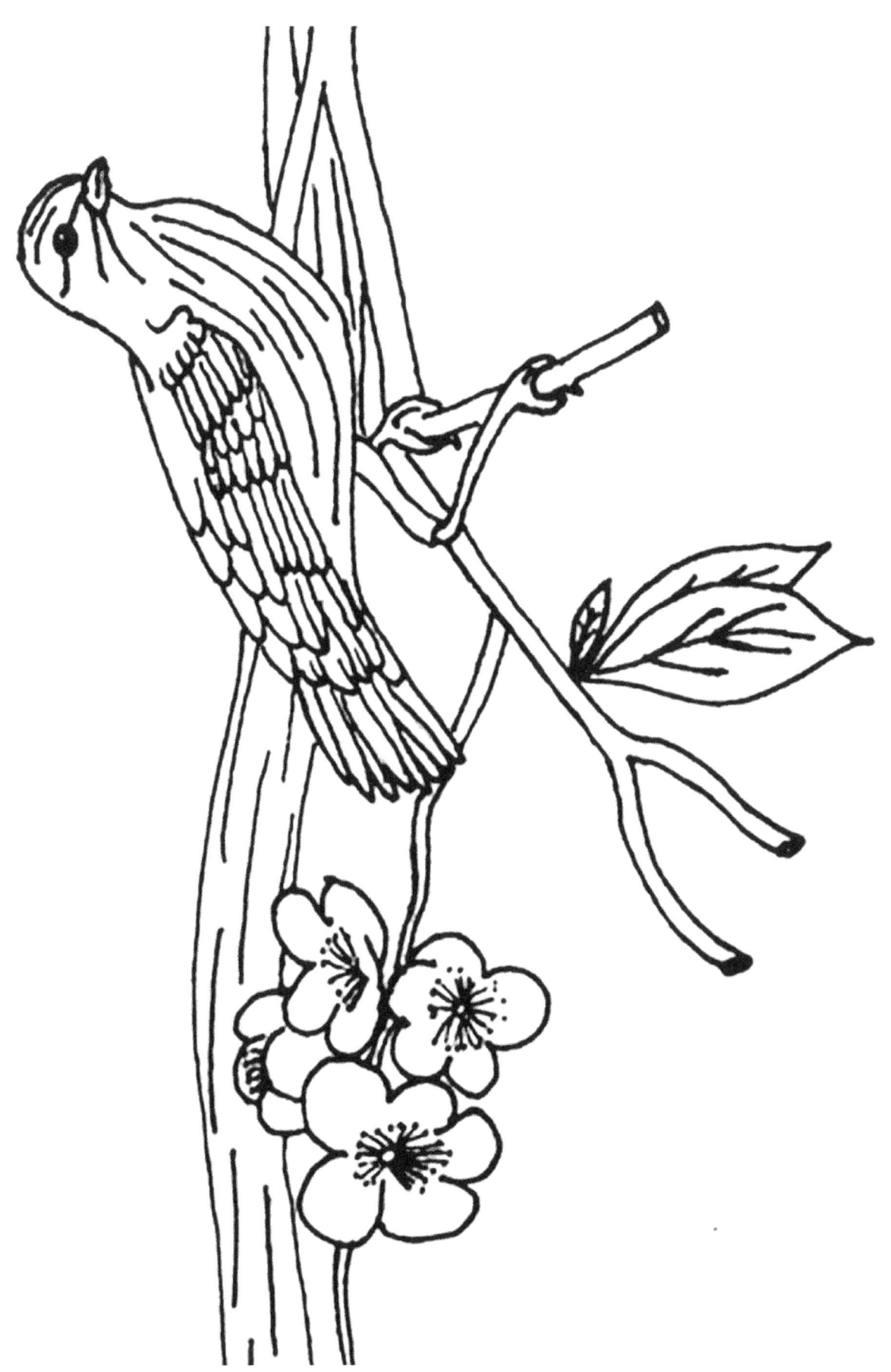

"Crataegus Punctata"

Patrick Reilly
Freshman

Teacher: Sarah Luttrell
Waynesville High School
Waynesville, Missouri

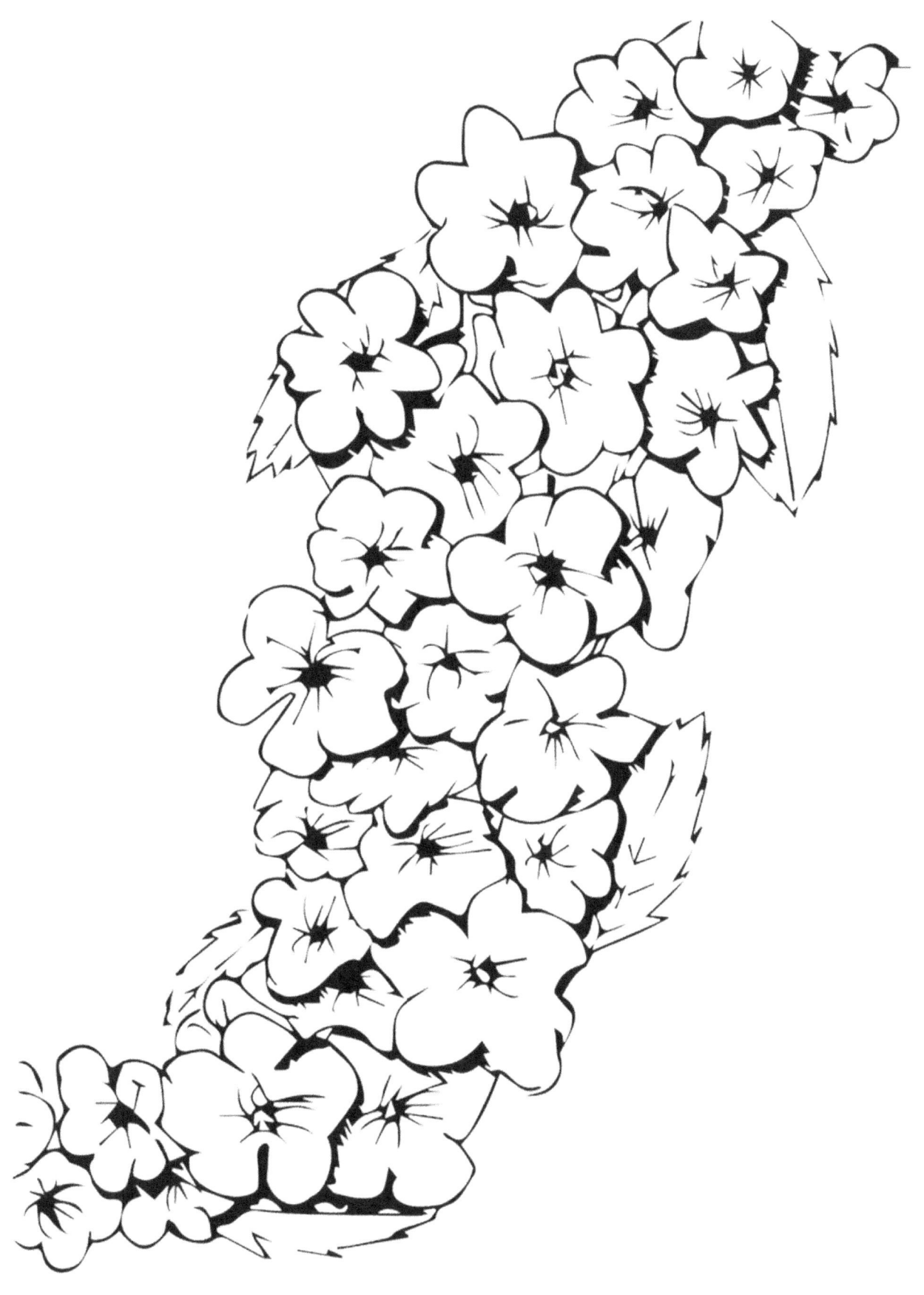

"Hypsibema Missouriense"

Adrian Hufford
Sophmore

One of the few official state dinosaurs, bones of the species were discovered in 1942, at what later became known as the Chronister Dinosaur Site near Glen Allen, Missouri. The remains of *Hypsibema missouriensis* at the site, which marked the first known discovery of dinosaur remains in Missouri, are the only ones to have ever been found. Although first thought to be a sauropod, later study determined that it was a hadrosaur, or "duck-billed" dinosaur, whose snouts bear likeness to ducks' bills. Some of the species' bones found at the Chronister Dinosaur Site are housed in Washington, D.C. Smithsonian Institution.

Teacher: Sarah Luttrell
Waynesville High School
Waynesville, Missouri

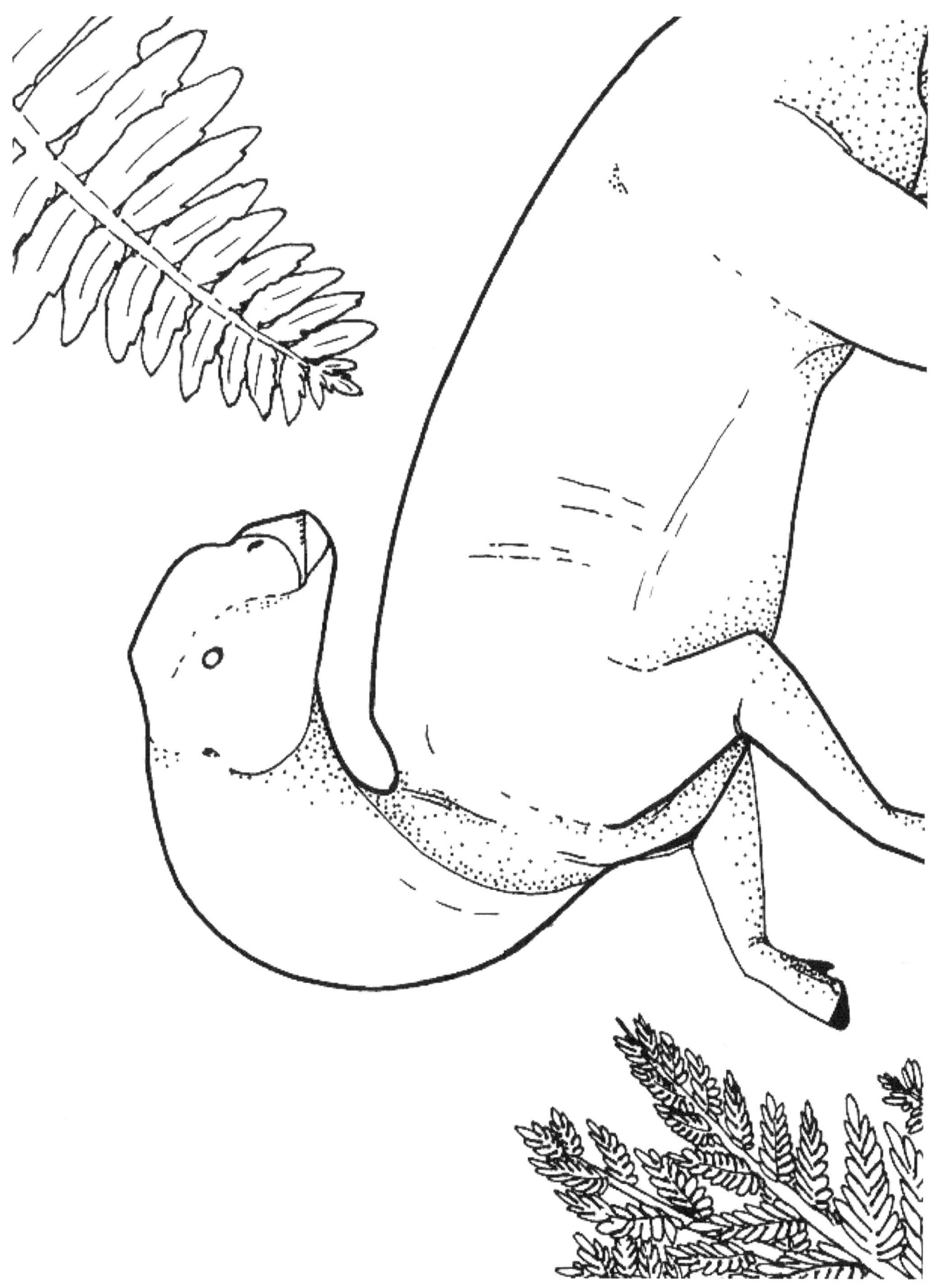

"Missouri Catfish & Wicker Basket"

Emmett Skinner
Junior

The artwork is of the Missouri fish, Catfish jumping out of the water behind the O of MO. In the background is the basket design.

Teacher: Sarah Luttrell
Waynesville High School
Waynesville, Missouri

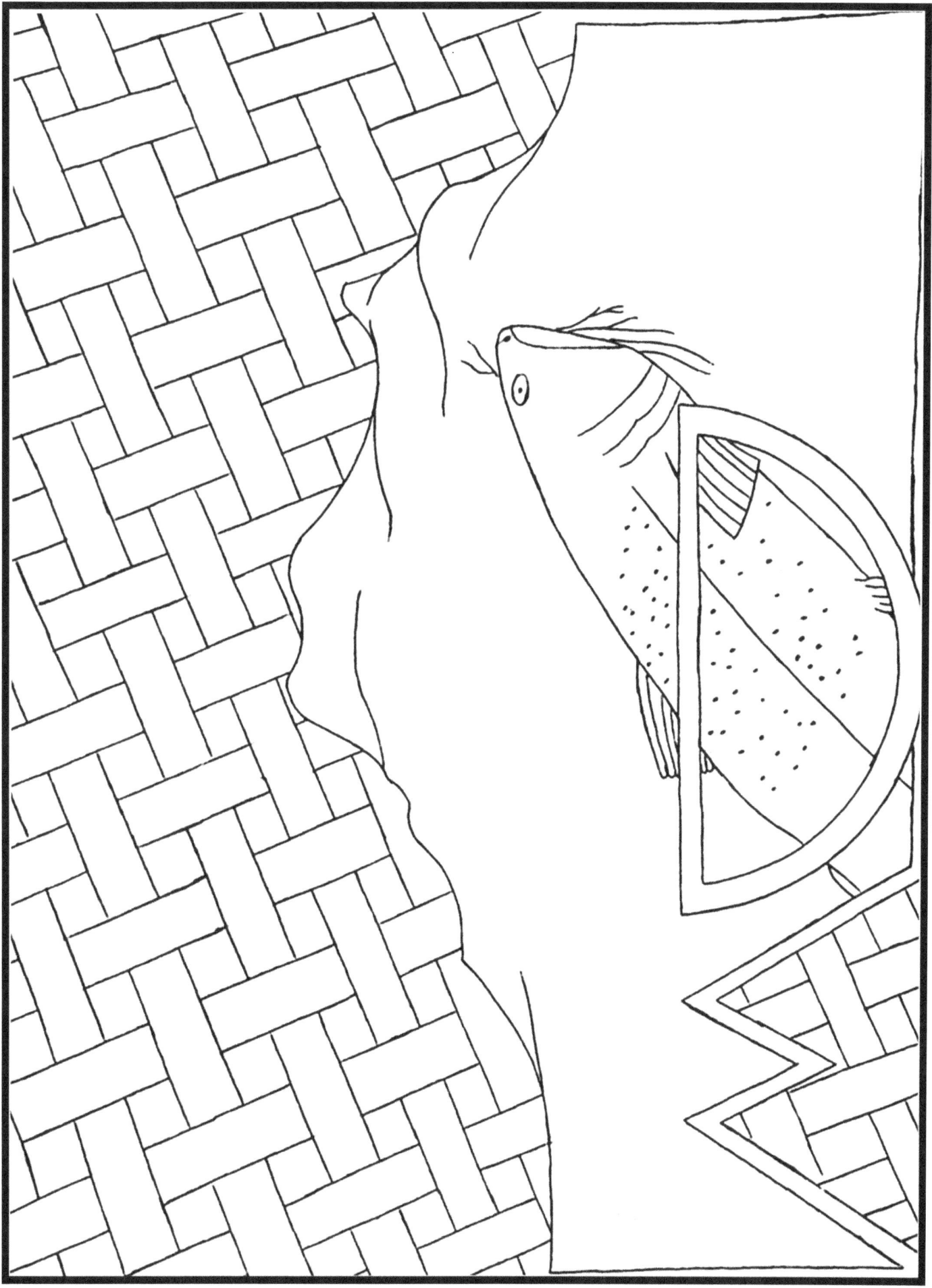

"Hawthorne"

Kaelyn Warson
Age: 15

Missouri state flower, the Hawthorne

Teacher: Sarah Luttrell
Waynesville High School
Waynesville, Missouri

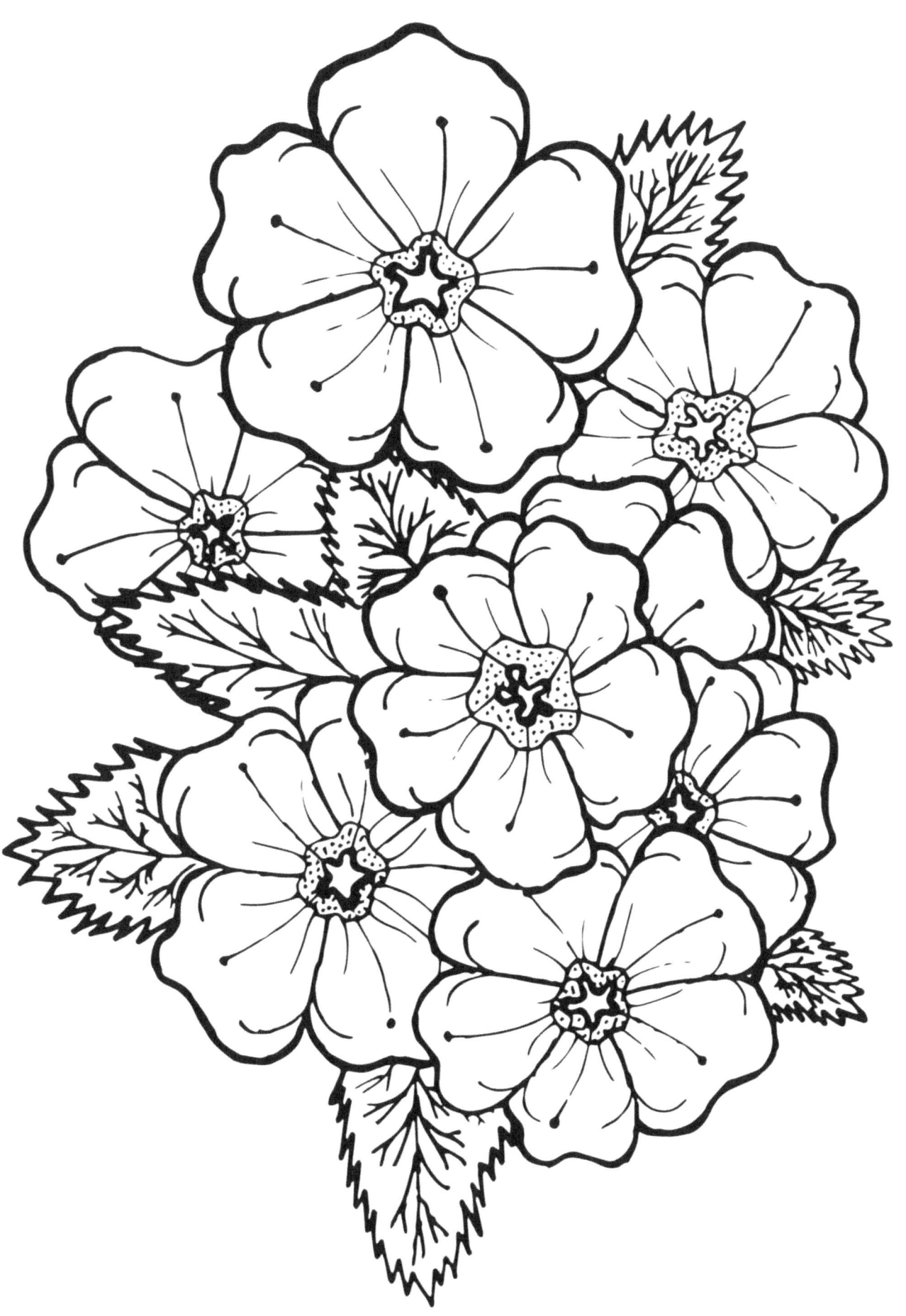

"1904 World's Fair"

Rani McCullough

The 1904 Worlds Fair in St. Louis was the site of the invention of many foods
we love and enjoy today: hamburgers, hotdogs, ice cream cones, and iced tea
to name a few

Teacher: Tina Hyde
Marshfield High School
Marshfield, Missouri

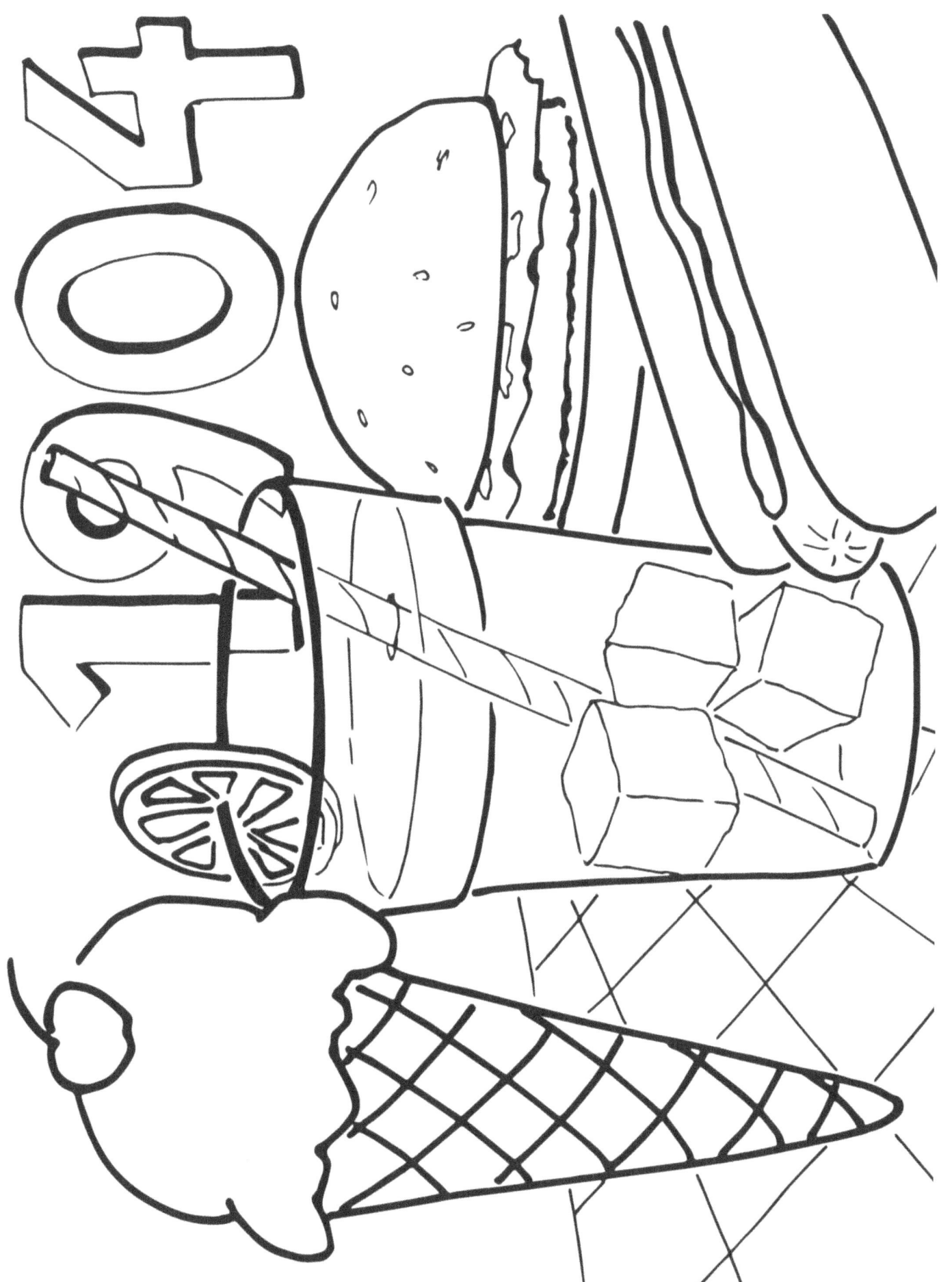

"Lets Go on a Picnic!"

Shayne Leary

There are many wonderful sites throughout the state of Missouri to have a picnic.

Teacher: Tina Hyde
Marshfield High School
Marshfield, Missouri

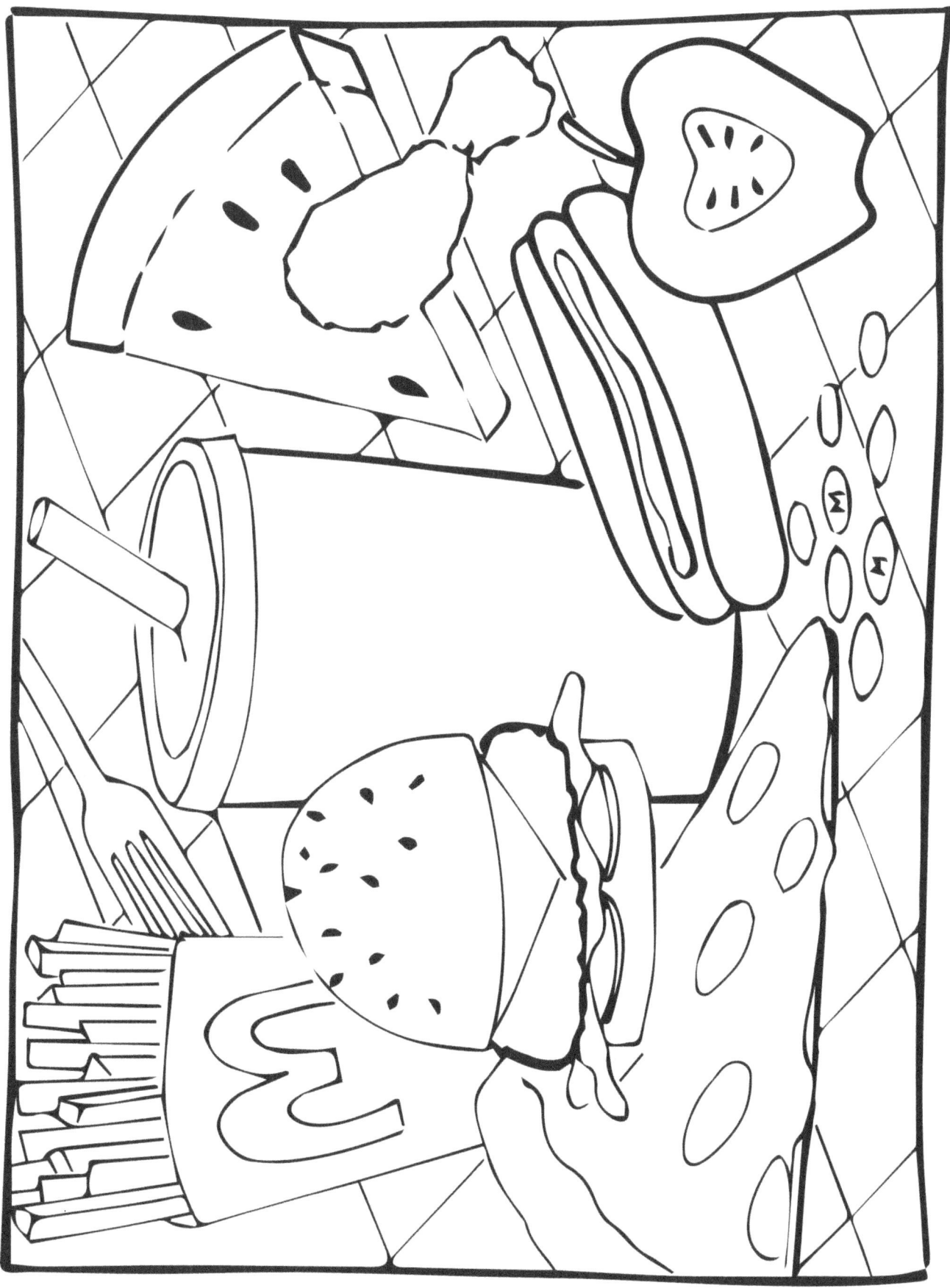

"Silver Dollar City"

Lauren Cartee
Senior

Teacher: Tina Hyde
Marshfield High School
Marshfield, Missouri

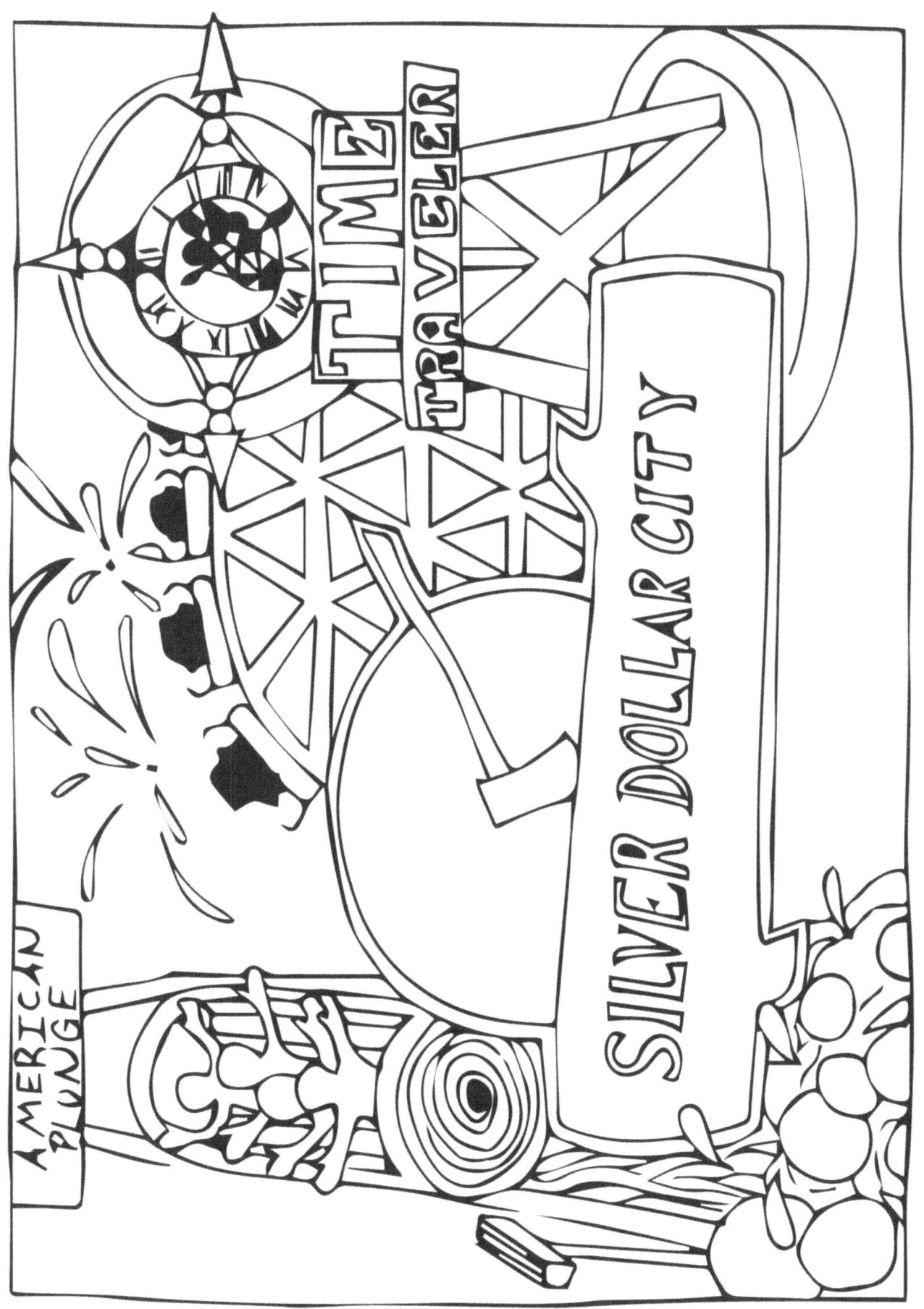

"Hawthorn"

Deanna Chapman
Junior

Teacher: Tina Hyde
Marshfield High School
Marshfield, Missouri

"Untitled"

Peyton Ward
6th Grade

Teacher: Mrs. Cherie Peters
Richland R-IV Elementary
Richland, Missouri

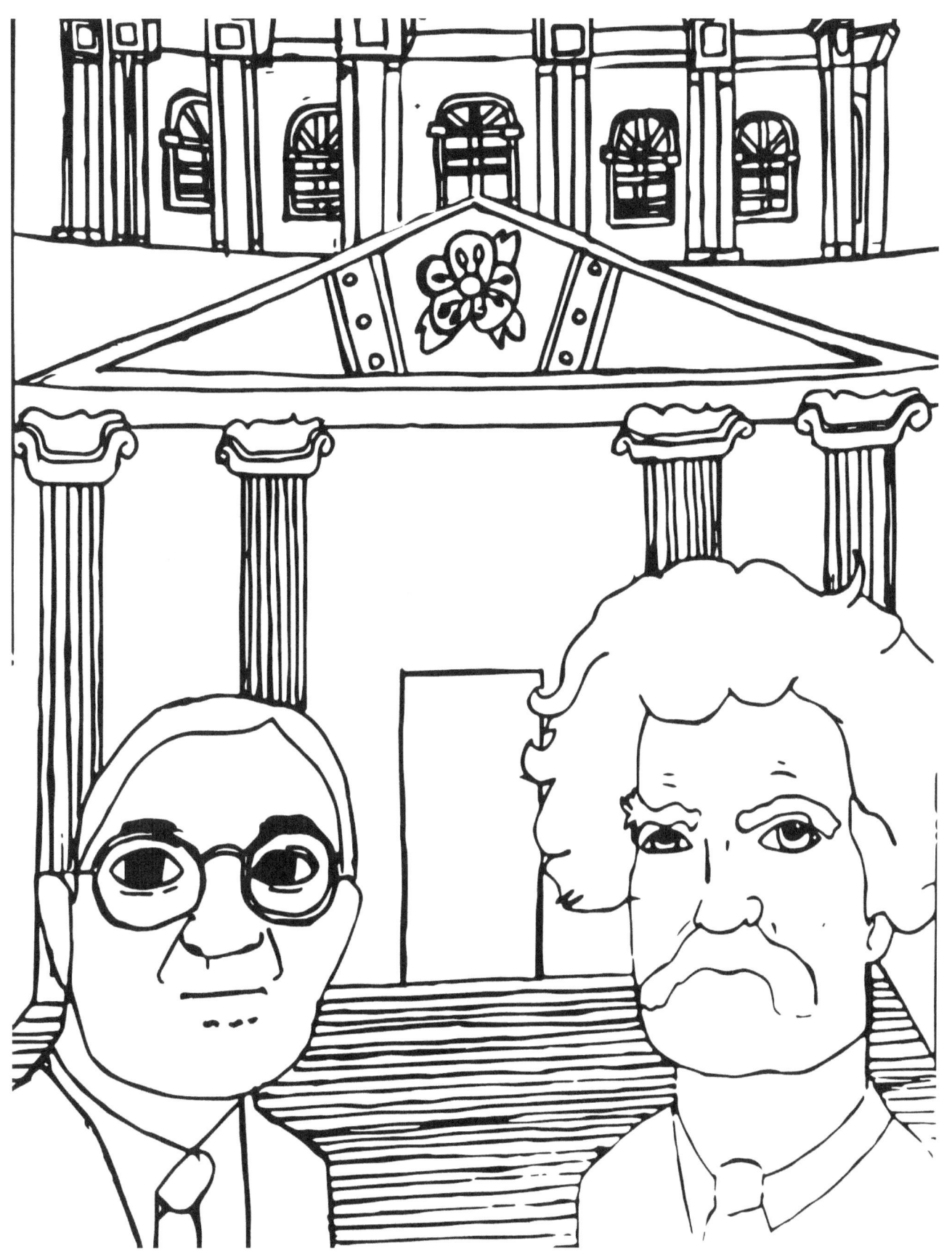

"Missouri State Flower & Blue Bird"

Ashley Rollins

Teacher: David Mitchell
S.C.O.R.E. Of Nixa Public Schools
Nixa, MO

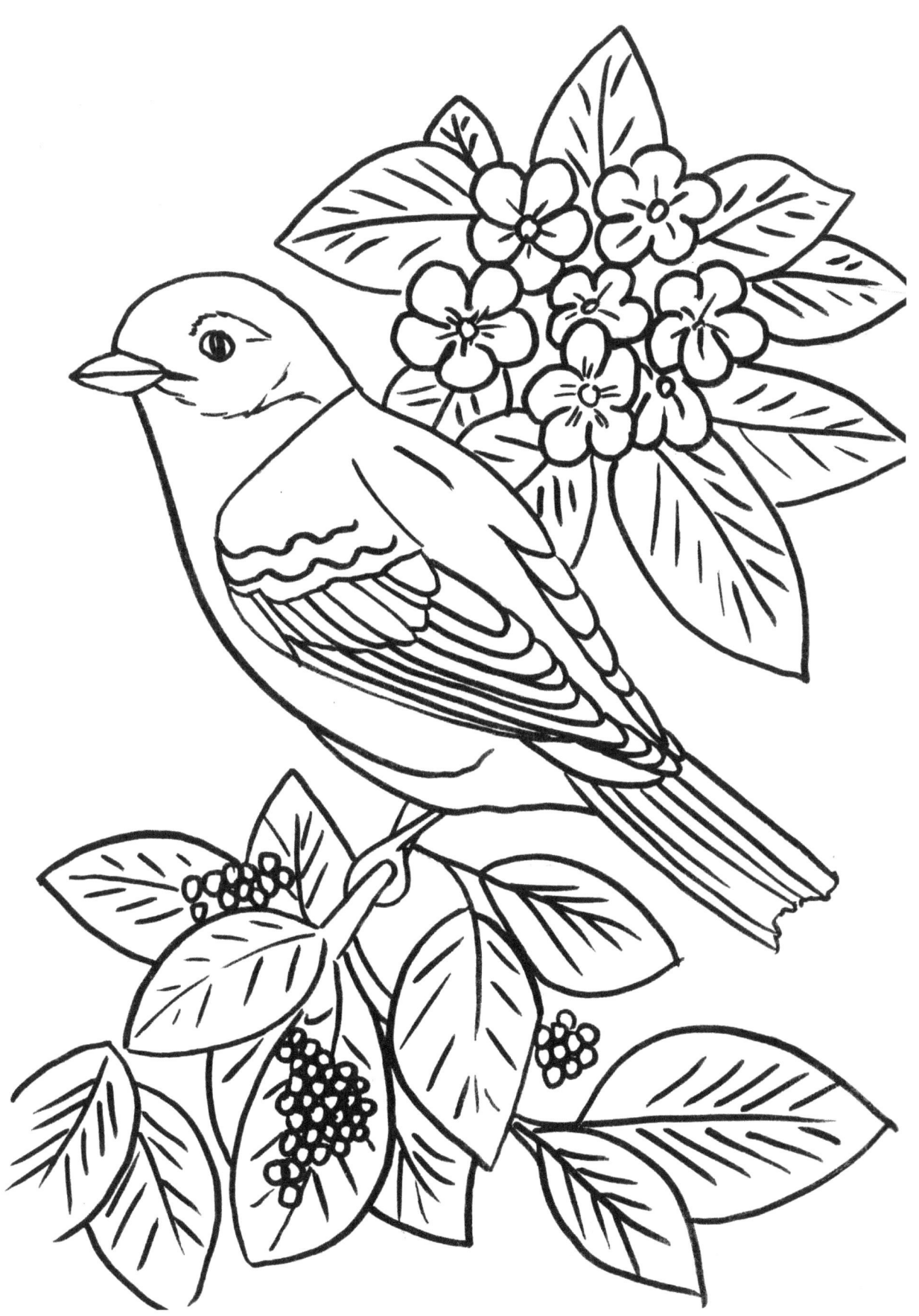

"Untitled"

Vanessa Hernandez
Senior 2020

Teacher: Dustin Miller
Neosho High School, Neosho, MO

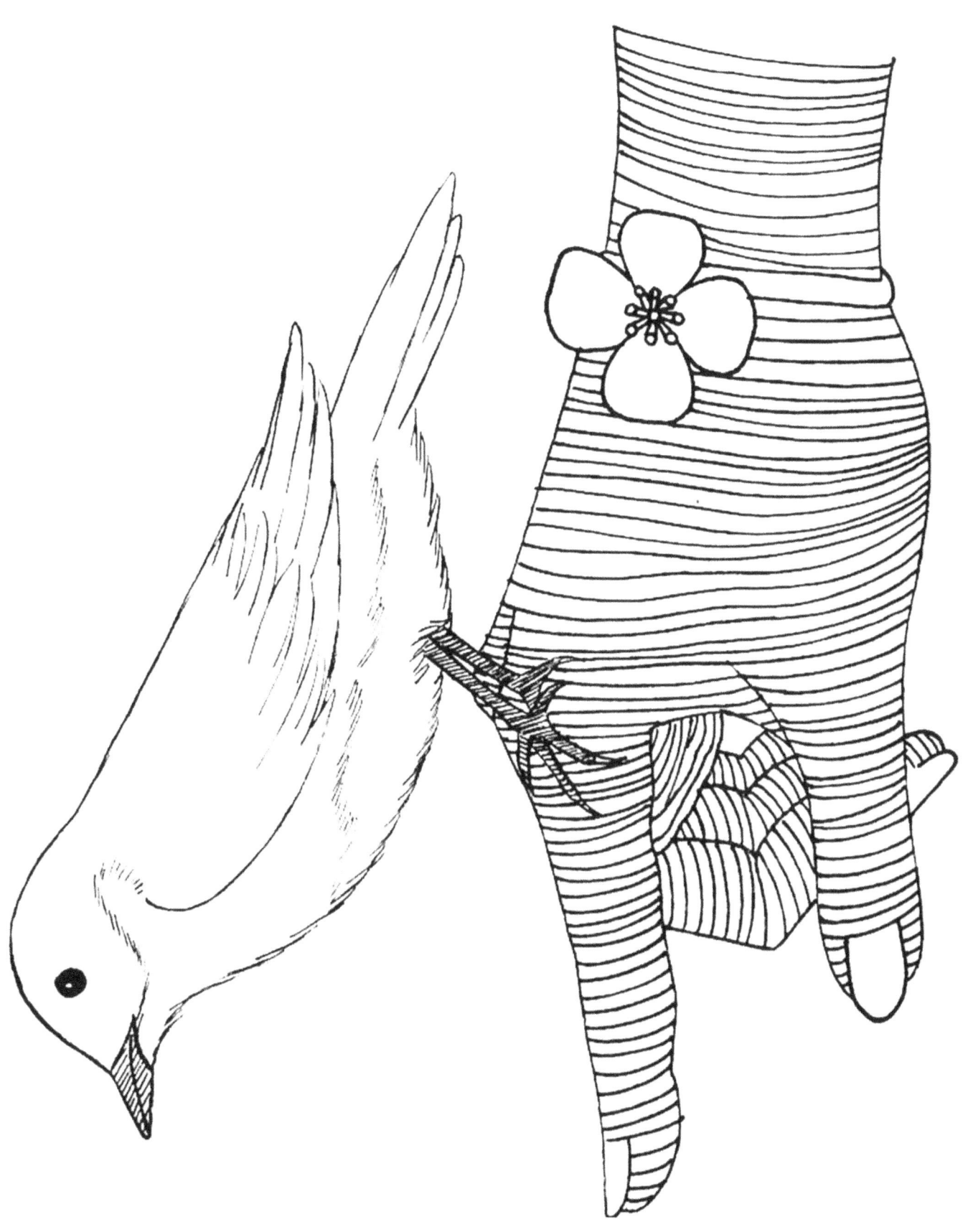

" Brown Trout, Northern Studfish, & Bigmouth Buffalo"

A Collage of 5th Grade Students fish

Connor Schooler

The Brown Trout is a game fish that isn't native to Missouri. It came from Europe and is released in Missouri from hatcheries.

Evan Kufahl

The Northern Studfish is known as an aggressive fish that can leap out of water when attacked. The males can become electric blue with orange, red and black patterns.

Daisy Williams

The Bigmouth Buffalo is Missouri's largest sucker fish. It can grow up to 48 inches long.

Teacher: Mrs. Rhonda Sexton
Disney Elementary
Springfield Public Schools
Springfield, Missouri

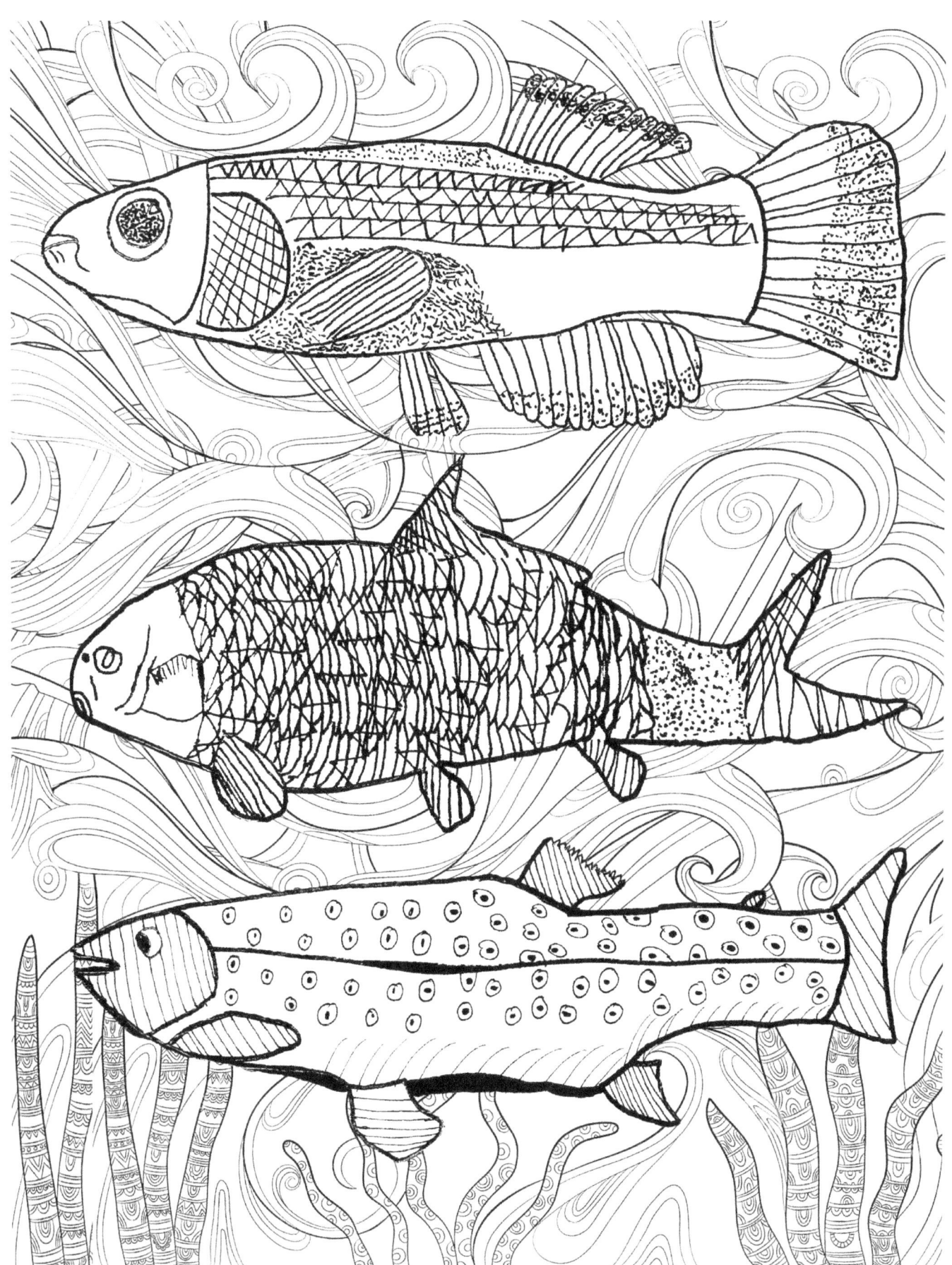

Largemouth Bass, Bluegill & River Carpsucker

Lilly Duda

Grade Level: 4

The Bluegill perch is found across almost all of Missouri's lakes, streams and rivers. It is one of the most common fish to panfry in North America.

Isaac White

The River Carpsucker can live up to 10 years and prefers murky rivers and streams.

Journey Shepherd

The Largemouth Bass is a carnivore and eats other fish, crawdads, big insects and will even eat other animals that fall into the water, like mice or snakes.

Teacher: Mrs. Rhonda Sexton
Disney Elementary
Springfield Public Schools
Springfield, Missouri

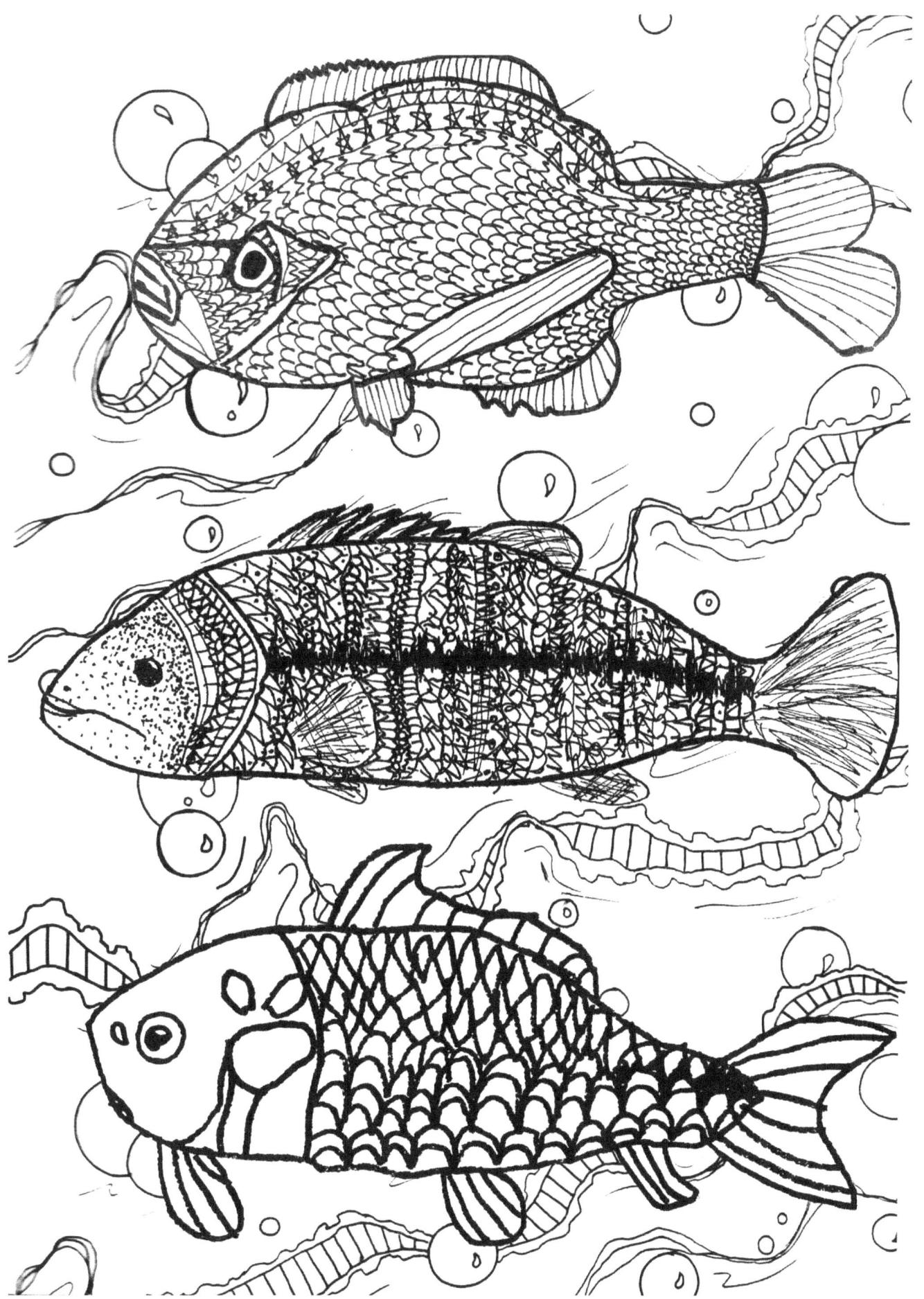

Black stripe Topminnow & Bighead Carp

Benjamin Hofius

The Black stripe Topminnow lives in Missouri's streams and is light brown in color.

Juliet Howes

The Bighead Carp is a bottom feeder so his eye is low on his head. He is not native to Missouri and comes from eastern Asia.

Teacher: Mrs. Rhonda Sexton
Disney Elementary
Springfield Public Schools
Springfield, Missouri

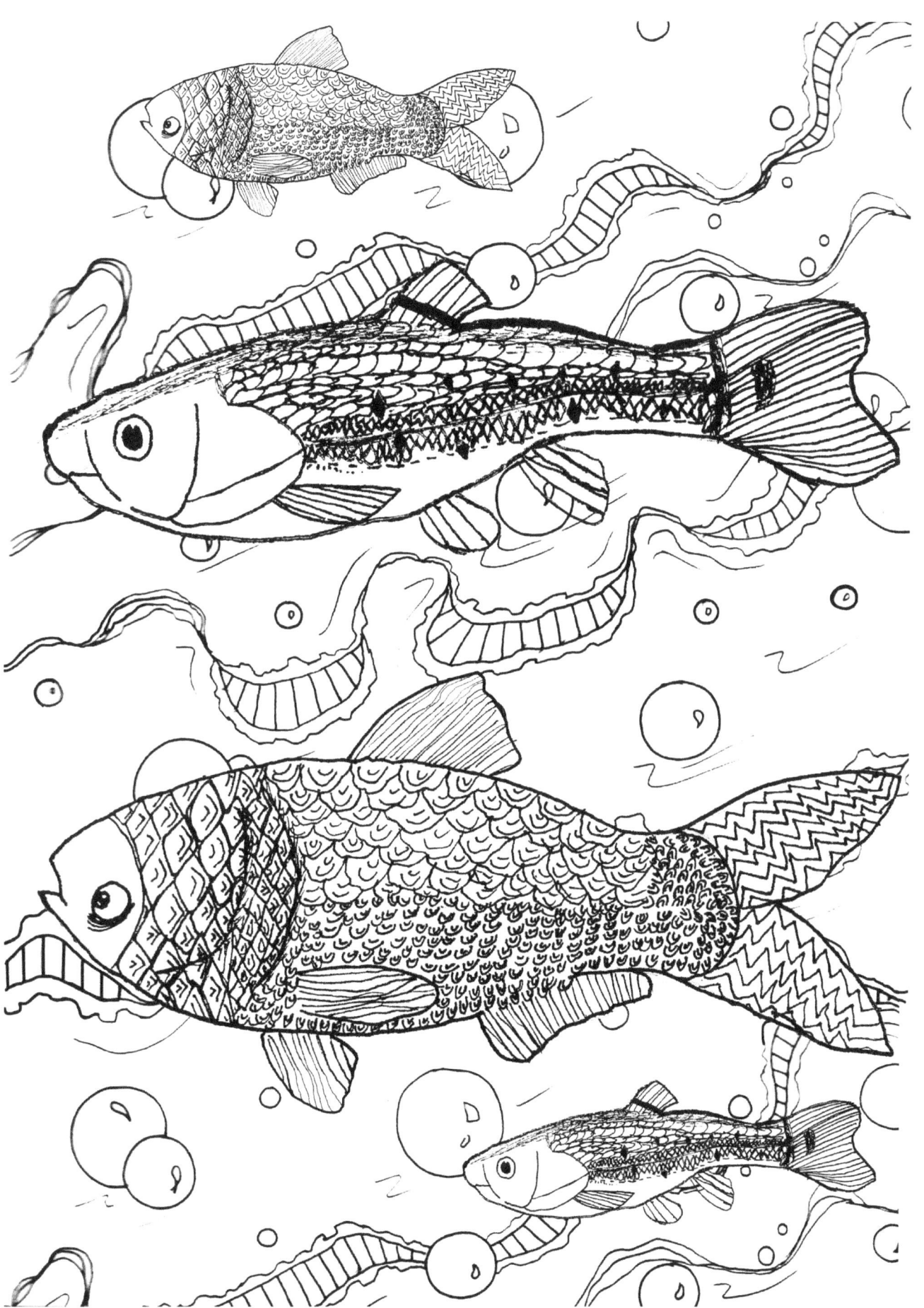

"Deer, Dogwoods, and Hawthorns"

Mariela Saldivar
Senior

Artist statement:

The idea behind this artwork was Missouri's beautiful nature. I infused the state flower, a white hawthorn blossom, and the state tree, a flowering Dogwood, into a common animal seen in Missouri. I wanted my piece to have a fantasy aspect to it which gave me the idea to morph the deer's antlers into Dogwood branches, then added the hawthorns as finishing touches.

Teacher: Cheryl Church
Carthage High School, Carthage

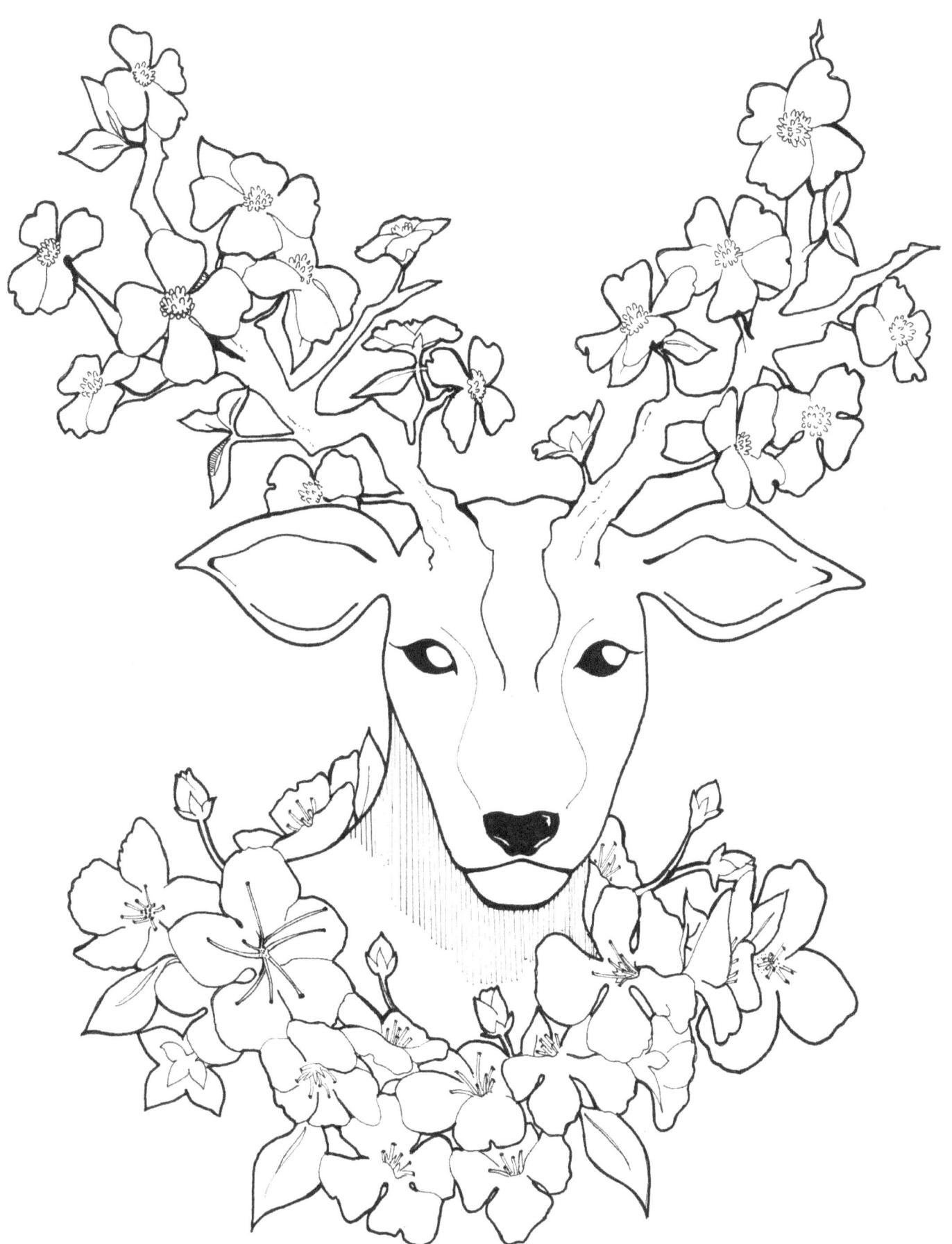

Thank you for
Supporting the
Arts of Missouri